W9-BKD-074

17.80

DEATH·BEFORE·DISHONOUR

DEATH·BEFORE·DISHONOUR
THE TRUE STORY OF FIGHTING MAC

—————→ TREVOR ROYLE ←—————

St. Martin's Press
New York

Library of Congress Catalog Card Number 82-61188

Design by James Hutcheson

First Edition

Grateful acknowledgement is given to the following for permission for illustrations to be reproduced in this book. Edinburgh City Libraries, 7; Illustrated London News, 4, 6, 10, 12, 25; National Army Museum, 5, 11, 14, 21; National Library of Scotland, 2, 3, 8, 24; Scottish National Portrait Gallery, 15; BBC Hulton Picture Library, 1, 16, 17, 18; Imperial War Museum, 22.

Printed and bound in Great Britain
by Spectrum Printing Company, Edinburgh

Contents

There were our own, there were the others.
Therefore, minding the great word of Glencoe's
son, that we should not disfigure ourselves
with villainy of hatred; and seeing that all
have gone down like curs into anonymous silence,
I will bear witness for I knew the others.
Seeing that littoral and interior are alike indifferent
and the birds are drawn again to our welcoming north
why should I not sing *them*, the dead, the innocent?

From *First Elegy: End of a Campaign*, by Hamish Henderson

Preface

This is not a regular biography of Major-General Sir Hector Macdonald, for being neither a diarist nor a voluminous correspondent, he left little in the way of primary evidence. Rather it is a biographical investigation of the life and times of a man who rose from the ranks to become an officer and a popular Victorian hero, who covered himself with glory fighting in some of Queen Victoria's little wars of Empire, and who died under most mysterious circumstances at the height of his career. In writing this book, I have been constantly aware that others have gone before me, and I have been particularly helped by John Montgomery's study, *Toll for the Brave*, which goes out of its way to illuminate Macdonald's relationship to Kitchener and to the military high command; and Kenneth I.E. Macleod's two pamphlets, *The Ranker* and *A Victim of Fate*, have been most useful in confirming the Ceylon evidence. Other sources are listed in the bibliography and chapter notes.

I owe a particular debt to Bill Campbell and Peter MacKenzie of Mainstream, my publishers, and to Ken Vass of STV, all of whom encouraged me to write this book, and to STV who commissioned me to write and present a documentary film on Macdonald to coincide with its publication. The film's director, Archie McArthur, his assistant Moira Nicol and the programme's researcher, Kate Comfort, who also supplied the illustrations, have all been towers of strength throughout the project.

My thanks are due to five people who gave of their time and patience on specialist matters or who helped with the loan of papers and books. Major-General Frank Richardson and Dr Jenny Eastwood supplied material on male sexuality; ex-Provost Alex MacRae of Dingwall made an extended loan of the invaluable Foulis scrapbook which was kept by Miss Munro of Foulis Castle; Robin Morgan, Principal of Daniel Stewart's and Melville College, Edinburgh, advised on small arms and the weapons of the Victorian army; and Mrs William Mackenzie of Rootfield, the general's niece, showed me some of Macdonald's papers and personal possessions. Over the years I have benefitted, too, from conversations and correspondence with others who have been interested in the story of 'Fighting Mac', namely Melvyn Harris, Edgar Lustgarten, Kay Mathieson, John Montgomery, John Vass, James Wilson, and the officers and men of the 1st battalion, the Gordon Highlanders. No book including information about August von Mackensen, the man whose identity Macdonald was rumoured to have taken, could have been written without the help of my old friend, Knut Mackensen, the field-marshal's grand-nephew.

I am grateful to Hamish Henderson for permission to allow me to quote from his first elegy taken from *Elegies for the Dead in Cyrenaica*, published in a new edition by EUSPB in 1977.

For help and advice in tracing official papers and in finding references from earlier studies, I wish to thank the staffs of the National Library of Scotland; Edinburgh City Libraries; Inverness Public Library; the Public Record Office, Kew; the National Army Museum, Chelsea; and the Gordon Highlanders' Museum, Aberdeen.

Lastly, it has not been without significance to me that my great-grandfather, Jonas Page, was in Roberts's Kabul Field Force when Macdonald made his well-nigh miraculous transition from the ranks to the officers' mess.

1

Two Lives or One?

It's almost possible to put an exact date on an obsession that has stamped in and out of my life for the past twenty years. Mid-June, 1962. I had stepped off the overnight boat from the Hook of Holland after spending a few memorable schoolboy weeks at the Kieler Gelehrtenschule in Kiel, in North Germany. As we thronged along the Harwich Parkeston Quay railway station, newspapers and magazines were hurriedly bought for the long journey home, north, to St Andrews in distant Scotland. Somehow—even to this day I have failed to explain its presence, because it certainly was not a Sunday—a copy of the *Sunday Express* fell into my lap.

Idly flicking through its pages, a headline jumped out at me: DID A SCOTS GENERAL LEAD THE KAISER'S ARMY? Written by Edgar Lustgarten, the barrister-writer and broadcaster who specialised in real-life criminal mysteries, it posed a sensational argument: that a crofter's son who had risen from the ranks to become a general in the British army and an *aide-de-camp* to Queen Victoria, had faked his suicide in 1903 and had taken the identity of a German officer who was destined to become a Field-Marshal in the Imperial German Army of Kaiser Wilhelm II and to die in Celle in 1945 at the grand old age of ninety-seven. The general's name was Sir Hector Archibald Macdonald, late of the 92nd (Gordon) Highlanders, more popularly known throughout the British army as 'Fighting Mac'; and the man whose identity he was supposed to have assumed was Field-Marshal Anton Ludwig Friedrich August von Mackensen, a dashing Hussar officer whose name was to be made during the First World War for the verve of his operations on the eastern and Balkan fronts.

"A whopping lie?" asked Lustgarten. "That wouldn't be a novel German characteristic either in domestic or external propaganda. But usually their lies have an ascertainable object. What would be the object of a lie like this?" The story had all the hallmarks of Lustgarten's probing, though excitable, legal style and it put much emphasis on a German document which was alleged to have been dropped on the Western Front during the First World War, claiming, "that one of our most famous commanders was born a Scottish peasant". Other coincidences were thrown in for good measure. The military records of both officers were submerged in official secrecy, or, more simply, were not available for the inquisitive. Macdonald had committed suicide in Paris in March 1903 under somewhat bizarre circumstances, and had been buried hurriedly in Edinburgh at the early morning hour of six o'clock. He had been learning German and during his last few months as military governor of Ceylon had spent some time engaged in books dealing with German military tactics and history. Lustgarten even went so far as to hint that Macdonald had spent his last hours in the company of a German military attaché and that the suicide had been faked, that rumour had it that 'Fighting Mac' "had gone over to the Hun". And to crown both his evidence and the startling nature of the article, the *Sunday Express* printed "the two faces that make it possible"—on the left Macdonald and opposite him von Mackensen. The faces immediately gripped my attention, because the portrait on the right was none other than that of *der alte Feldmarschal,* the grand-uncle of my host in Kiel.

I had met one of his sons, a Second World War general, and Knut, my schoolfellow and host in Kiel, the grand-nephew of the field-marshal, was imbued in the history and mythology of that proud Prussian military family. Stories about that venerable old character had helped to lift my stay in Germany from the ordinary to the legendary, and what stories they had been! The field-marshal had fought as a subaltern in the Franco-Prussian War of 1871, his exploits during the First World War verged on the heroic and the fact that he had survived to outlive Germany's destruction for a second time in thirty years was mentioned with a sense of honour and not a little pride. His death at the age of ninety-seven, claimed Knut, had nothing to do with natural causes but was due to the fact that he had been forbidden to don his famous black Death's Head Hussar uniform. During the nineteen-twenties when the *mark* became so devalued as to be utterly worthless, he had been forced to ride into town post-haste in a carriage filled with his pension and to spend it quickly before inflation took a further toll. Perhaps it was because of that hungry experience, he was able to boast convincingly that his waistline had not changed from subaltern to field-marshal.

In the hateful period that followed the lean nineteen-twenties he remained *kaisertreu* and although, no doubt, he was pleased to see the rejuvenation of the German army under Corporal Hitler, like other aristocratic officers, he despised the petty, mean, low-born Nazis. Everywhere I had looked in the Mackensen family album, his presence had been felt. Proudly sitting on a white charger. A smiling *pater familias*, secure within the bourne of a large, loving family. An august figure at state occasions, all polished boots, silver trappings and the stern face beneath the whitened skull of the Death's Head Hussar's busby. More than anything else, though, it had been the circle of his family in the photographs that had impressed me—the family likenesses in the faces of the sons and the other relatives, the sheer domesticity of it all.

Lustgarten's story haunted me all the way back to St Andrews, and a few days later I wrote indignantly to the author, pointing out the impossibility of a fifty-year old Scot taking the place of an aristocratic Prussian with five grown-up children. How could a cover-up so gross and so clumsily thought up have been engineered, even by a country as wily as Germany was supposed to be? (And even by the early nineteen-sixties, as I had discovered, memories of the war were still to the fore in Germany and Britain.) No, the whole matter was clearly a piece of sensational journalism.

The reply from Edgar Lustgarten was cool and polite. It was the absence of hard facts, he explained, together with the web of rumour and innuendo, that made the Macdonald story so fascinating. He was merely postulating a theory and there the matter would have to remain. (Later I was to find that much of Lustgarten's evidence came from an article written for *Blackwood's Magazine,* and to take the coincidences a stage farther, it was for that magazine that I was to work on leaving university in 1968.) But it was impossible to take his well-meant advice.

Von Mackensen, it was true, was a shadowy figure to British eyes. Because he had not fought on the Western Front his name lacked the household coinage of a Hindenberg or a Ludendorff, and in the histories dealing with the period he emerged as a remote and ethereal figure, one who had done his best for the Fatherland in a theatre of war that seemed to have had little bearing on the outcome of the hostilities. At court he was known for his high-stepping chivalry and for introducing the habit of kissing the Kaiser's hand, a habit which many Teutons of fiercer mien found to be distasteful, smacking as it did of French decadence or Ruritanian melodrama. From the family I heard that of all the senior officers at the Kaiser's court, von Mackensen had remained the truest and when Wilhelm was laid to rest in lonely exile in Holland, the aged field-marshal wept openly before throwing his riding cloak over the dead king's coffin.

All things considered, he was a far more satisfactory hero than Macdonald, a mere major-general who seemed to be little more than

a footnote to history's pages. A glance at the available biographies—
standard Edwardian *Boys' Own* hagiographies—seemed only to
confirm his honest, good-natured endeavour in distant parts of
the British Empire. Besides, Lustgarten had hinted that he was a
homosexual and with all the priggishness that adolescence can be
heir to, that seemed to warrant a halt to further interest in him.

It was only when I was in a pub in Perth a year later that I began to
change my mind. While re-telling the strange saga of August von
Mackensen, an old man, ex-Black Watch and a survivor of the First
World War, turned to me and said that, yes, indeed, von Mackensen
was none other than 'Fighting Mac' of the Gordons. It had been, he
added, a well-known fact on his sector of the Western Front during
the First Battle of Ypres that 'Fighting Mac' had "gone across to the
Hun" and that he would never be used against his old comrades in
arms. Hence, as von Mackensen, he had been sentenced to languish
in some little-known part of Eastern Europe safely away from the
danger of conflicting loyalties. He went on to say that Macdonald was
still revered by the Scottish soldier, that his death had been rigged
and that he had been forced into treachery by the enmity of one of
his superiors, Earl Kitchener of Khartoum.

With several fine variations, I was to hear that same story again and
again over the coming years. 1963 also saw the publication of John
Montgomery's *Toll for the Brave: The Tragedy of Sir Hector Macdonald,* a
brief biography which provided a good deal of fresh insights into the
life and times of the crofter's son who was destined to rise through
the ranks to a position of authority and power within the caste-
ridden British army. Far from being a dull imperial policeman, Hector
Macdonald came alive as a shy, retiring man, an expert tactician who
earned the loyalty and respect, and in many quarters the admiration,
of his fellow countrymen for his military integrity and for his honest
courage. The more I looked at his life and career, and then stared
myopically into the mist of deceit that covered his death, the odder it
seemed that people in positions of authority presumably wanted the
whole affair to be hushed up.

How had it been possible for a senior and well-liked officer to have
been branded by unsubstantiated charges, to have committed suicide
in a sad hotel room in Paris and then to have been hastily buried,
without ceremony, in Edinburgh, five days later at a god-forsaken
hour of the morning? It seemed to be inconceivable that one of the
few officers to have emerged with honour from the Transvaal War
and from the Sudanese campaign of the eighteen-nineties should
have been committed to the earth with stealth and shame in
Scotland's capital. Suddenly Macdonald seemed to be very inter-

esting indeed.

His story had all the elements of tragedy. Raised too high from the obscurity of the ranks of a Highland regiment, his star deserted him when he began to threaten those in positions of authority, those whose rank was a birthright and not a hard-earned privilege. While it was true that other officers of the period—Field-Marshal Sir William Robertson is the prime example—won commissions from the ranks, it was unusual for the private soldier in the Victorian army to find room in his knapsack, if not for the marshal's coveted baton then at least for the general's scarlet jacket. Yet in spite of those handicaps, or perhaps in Hector's case because of them, Macdonald was the epitome of British pluck, a man who by dint of his own cool-headedness and courage had not only reached field rank but had also taken part in some of the most vicious fighting seen by the British army during Queen Victoria's little wars in the last quarter of the nineteenth century.

Then there were the legends that surrounded any mention of his name. During the Second Afghan War of 1878, when Lord Roberts raised a field force to avenge the death of the British resident in Kabul, Macdonald, then a colour sergeant with the Gordons, distinguished himself at the Shutargardan Pass and then at the Battle of Charasiah, and for his pains he was supposed to have been offered the choice of a Victoria Cross or a commission. Good servant of the regiment that he was, he chose the latter and was welcomed into the peculiarly family ambience of the officers' mess of a Highland regiment. Impossible, of course, but the story only served to fuel the legend of the man who was coming to be known as 'Fighting Mac'. At Majuba Hill, that disaster for Victorian military pride, he again covered himself with glory, holding a spur of the hill until the last round of ammunition and ending up by pummelling the advancing Boers with his bare fists. His sword—a gift from his brother Gordons—was taken from him on his surrender, but was later returned into his safe keeping, the Boer General Joubert remarking that, "A brave man and his sword should not be separated." In the Sudan he made his black Sudanese brigade the equal of any crack regiment in the British army, and by drilling them hard and treating them fairly and squarely he forged them into a fierce fighting force who were prepared to die for him to a man. Something of that loyalty was revealed during a long route march when Macdonald overheard three of his men plotting to shoot him in the back, come the first opportunity. Undaunted, he lined up the brigade and invited the soldiers three to carry out their threat.

"Now," he said, "you three fellows are going to shoot me when we are next fighting, are you? But why wait so long? Why not do it now? You have your rifles, why not use them? Here I am—shoot me." But the assembled ranks began to laugh. The three would-be assassins were shamed in front of their brothers and the incident passed without bloodshed. Of such stories are heroes made.

Given the mixture of so much romance and so much hard fact, Macdonald's life should have been celebrated with honour and pride, but when "grave charges" were brought against him while he was serving as commander of the British troops in Ceylon, his end was destined to be shabby and lacking in dignity. After the confused events of the suicide in Paris and the hasty burial in Edinburgh, Macdonald became something of a tragic hero in Scotland, broad hints being passed that it was the folk in the higher reaches of army command who had "stabbed him in the back". Although the memory of his career was to be dimmed by the maelstrom of the First World War, Fighting Mac was not altogether forgotten in Scotland and pockets of resistance continued to cherish his memory and persevered in their attempts to breach the wall of War Office silence.

There were also those who refused to believe that he had in fact died in Paris and while the von Mackensen myth was the most potent, as we shall see later, there were several other equally strong rumours about Macdonald's defection. Macdonald and von Mackensen were both fascinating, and in their different ways, unusual characters and the story of the swap is an attractive one, but it should not be allowed to obscure the facts of Hector's life. Similarly as I hope to show, many of the rumours and gossip that surround the events of the crucial days between the 25th and the 30th of March 1903, between the suicide and the burial, have been kept alive just to maintain the mystery. And Kitchener's role in the whole affair, while shadowy and insubstantial, is perhaps more subtle than the villainous part in which he is usually cast.

The Public Record Office papers referring to Macdonald, or more sensationally, their supposed absence, are not the obstacle that the idly inquisitive suppose them to be. There are ample references to him in the Kitchener and Roberts papers, his service record is available and in the Colonial Office papers there is the evidence of the telegrams and memos between Ceylon and the Foreign Office. What is missing is any firm evidence about the nature of the charges brought against him. It is their lack of substance that continues to haunt Fighting Mac, and over the years several people have attempted to exorcise the ghost in the machine. Apart from Montgomery's book, there have been two booklets on various aspects of the case, a stage play and two films (one of which I wrote for

Scottish Television). Of von Mackensen the only reliable guide to his life is Wolfgang Förster's *Briefe und Aufzeichungen* (1938), which is a splendid record of his career and campaigns through the evidence of his letters to people as different, though close to him, as his wife and his chief of staff. And, of course, there are still the photographs and other mementoes in Kiel.

My search for Hector Macdonald—which began all those years ago when I first came across the notion that he had two lives, not one,— has taken me back to the condition of Scotland during Hector's youth and also deep into the army background of his adult years and into the part that it played in maintaining Queen Victoria's world empire. It has also led to a new understanding of the line regiments of the British army, then as now, tightly-knit communities, with their own peculiar *lares et penates*. And from them, a picture emerges of what it was like to "go for a soldier" in the latter half of Victoria's reign.

All those elements have their parts to play in the story of a very unusual and gallant gentleman, Major-General Sir Hector Archibald Macdonald, K.CB., D.S.O., A.D.C., LL.D., the crofter's son who became a general, the darling of Scotland and acknowledged by one and all as the true hero of the Battle of Omdurman.

2

The Crofter's Son

At the height of his fame, English journalists liked to make much of the 'fact' that Fighting Mac had sprung from a long line of legendary Highland heroes and that the place of his birth, Mulbuie on the Black Isle in Easter Ross, was a Gaelic derivative meaning the 'isle of Mars'. The truth was rather more prosaic. He was born at Rootfield, a small croft or small-holding, tenanted by his father from the estate of J.F. Mackenzie of Allangrange in the parish of Ferintosh and Urquhart, which stands on a long, spine-like ridge of the Black Isle, running from the Muir of Ord to the town of Cromarty at its eastern extension. Known as Mulbuie, or Milbuie (a Gaelic derivative certainly, but not the martial isle dreamt up by Edwardian journalists—it means the yellow mount or headland), it is today partially forested and modern methods of farming and husbandry have brought a new prosperity to its once sour and rocky soil. The land is steeped in antiquity with many chambered cairns bearing mute witness to the area's prehistoric importance and to its attraction to Bronze Age men, and down the years the Black Isle has played a significant part in the history of the Moray Firth. Today, oil-related developments at nearby Nigg and the industrialisation of the Alness-Invergordon section have altered the calm of centuries and brought with them new housing, improved roads and an increased population but even those cannot entirely disturb the isolation or remove the sense of space that continues to pervade the lands around the flanking Moray and Cromarty Firths, those yawning river estuaries that give Easter Ross its special character.

A good, fast, metalled road, taking its freight of population and goods on the direct route south to Inverness, runs past the road-end that leads to Rootfield West, past the cylindrical monument erected to Macdonald by his schoolfellows, and the still extant schoolhouse of his childhood, but little else has changed in the natural scenery. Instead of the ribbon development of the crofts of former years, the farms are larger now, more prosperous looking than they would have been one hundred and fifty years ago. Despite its modernisation, it is possible to see in the farmhouse of Rootfield something of the shape of the modest house that belonged to William Macdonald, the tenant farmer who welcomed his seventh son into the world on a cold Spring's morning, the fourth of March, 1853. (In later life, Macdonald's birth was given frequently as 13th April 1852, but this was doubtless due to the fact that in 1870, when he joined the army, he told a white lie to the recruiting sergeant so that he would not have to wait another year before taking the Queen's shilling.)

The weather was bitterly unseasonal, even for the early Highland Spring that has to fight to free itself from the grudging months of the northern winter. Hard frost held the ground in a vice-like grip and all around, the country was covered by a blanket of snow, as far as the eye could see, across the firth to the bulky shoulders of distant Ben Wyvis. Contemporary accounts commented on the severity of the storm that had swept over the countryside bringing havoc in its wake and casting up huge drifts of snow in the narrow, ill-kept country roads. March had, indeed, come in like a lion, and William Macdonald remembered, not without a sense of awe, that the weather was extraordinarily similar to the bitterly cold, storm-tossed days of his own wedding day, nine years earlier.

An Inverness-shire man, William Macdonald had been forced by circumstance to work as a stonemason and drystane dyker to help eke out a living for his parents, and it was on one of his expeditions to other parts of the county that he had met his wife, Ann Boyd, while he was engaged in building a farm steading at Killiechoilum in Stratherrick, in the uplands of Foyne near Inverness. They married in the winter of 1844 and for the rest of their life together they worked hard at the small croft of Rootfield, slowly improving it year by careful year, until it became a pretentious farm of some sixty acres. But during the early years of their marriage, the crofting community of Mulbuie was poor and disorganised. Living in small farming units, from which they could be easily and ruthlessly evicted at a landlord's whim, they lacked the basic security and economic standing to expand their horizons and to build up their capacity to earn a decent living from the land. Communities like theirs straggled across Scotland from the north-east, through the Highlands, to the islands of the west, and, although they differed in terms of shape and size and in economic standing, the houses were basically similar in their level of poverty-stricken lack of comforts: "an old-fashioned farmhouse with offices attached, all thatched with straw and ropes, and situated on the south side of a hill . . . and having a morass or bog . . . to the south . . . at one end stood the byres and at the other the stable and kiln-barn, with a dung-hill in the centre".[1] The description of their childhood home in Banffshire by the brother of the Victorian photographer, George Washington Wilson, could equally well have applied to the Mulbuie of Hector's boyhood.

It was only as the old ties of clanship began to loosen with the consequent re-organisation of the land available for farming that the crofters were encouraged to expand their holdings in order to uphold the landlords' vision of farming as a competent capitalist enterprise. William Macdonald owed his fortune, no doubt, to energy and good luck, but only one of his sons could inherit the farm (it was to be the third son, also called William), and he lived to see his children take the road south, to earn their livings elsewhere: Hector to the army and his brothers to Australia, London, and Devon. That was a common enough expectation and it was understood from an early age that all the boys would have to leave home once they reached man's estate. Until then each child was supposed to pay his way and much of Hector's childhood was spent in the hard darg of farm labour.

At the age of six he was sent to the Mulbuie school to get what education was available and it was scant enough, even in a country that had prided itself on the universality of its parish education. The schoolhouse—which still stands a hundred yards or so away from a later, turn-of-the-century construction—was a long, low-ceilinged building, dark, with walls of bare stone and lime and with precious little in the way of equipment. The master stood behind a pulpit-like desk at one end of the room and in front of him sat his charges, of all ages and abilities, as he struggled to give them a grounding in basic literacy. In Hector's day, the master was a well-liked, simple, basically educated fellow called Alexander Treasurer who was to lose his job in 1870 when the Education Act of that year demanded stricter qualifications for country schoolmasters. He ended up working as a clerk for the North British Railway Company in Inverness but he lived to see the triumph of the Hector he remembered as a plodding boy who refused to be daunted by the mysteries of reading and writing. "A little thick-set fellow, whose head just topped the desk, he delighted in arithmetic, geography and history."[2] And even those basics would have been scantily enough taught, despite Treasurer's cautious encouragement.

The schoolmaster was also to remember Hector's delight in games and make-believe battles in which his gentle courage was always to the fore. While memory may be a great deceiver the image that stuck in Alexander Treasurer's mind at the height of his young charge's fame, was of his determination and personal bravery. "Well, I will say this for Hector. He did not swear like many of the other boys and he would never allow a big boy to bully a little one. Everything he undertook, he entered into with determination."[3] And other stories abounded too, in particular the story of the heroic battle between the boys from the northern part of the parish, led by young Hector and those from the south side led by an older boy, Donald McLennan. After the customary throwing of insults and clods of earth, battle commenced with the two gangs laying in to each other with whin sticks and old broom handles. Eventually parents were called in to break up the fray and there the matter would have ended had not Hector insisted on turning on Donald McLennan one last time because he had been called a coward.

Although Hector Macdonald left no record of his schooldays other than the platitudes of Alexander Treasurer and the rosier memories harboured by the men of Mulbuie in more successful days, something of the atmosphere of a Scottish village school can be felt in the autobiographical writings of Macdonald's fellow countryman of an earlier generation, the remarkable, self-taught geologist, Hugh Miller, who had been born in 1802 in the busy fishing and trading port of Cromarty which lies at the end of the Black Isle where the Moray Firth meets the sea.

> The building in which we met was a low, long, straw-thatched cottage, open from gable to gable, with a mud floor below, and an unlathed roof above; and stretching along the naked rafters, which, when the master chanced to be absent for a few minutes, gave noble exercise in climbing, there used frequently to lie a helm, or oar, or boathook, or even a foresail—the spoil of some hapless peat-boat from the opposite side of the Firth.[4]

And from that same autobiographical study, *My Schools and Schoolmasters*, Miller left a sketch of a country schoolmaster who could quite easily have been a prototype for Alexander Treasurer in Mulbuie at the other end of the Black Isle.

> The parish schoolmaster was a scholar and an honest man, and if a boy really wished to learn, *he* certainly could teach him. He had attended the classes in Aberdeen during the same sessions as the late Dr Mearns, and in mathematics and the languages had disputed the prize with the Doctor; but he had failed to get on equally well in the world; and now, in middle life, he had settled down to be what he subsequently remained, the teacher of a parish school.[5]

Although a generation divided them, there are several similarities between Miller and Macdonald, quite apart from the accident of the county of their birth. Each was destined to make a name for himself in the world and to gain the notice of the leaders of their age, and both were to experience the awkwardness of rising out of one class into another at a time when social mobility was not dissimilar to

crossing a minefield in no-man's land on a moonless night. They
forged their lives into their own creation, grasped Fortune's wheel
and turned it at the speed that suited them best. Very much Victorian
men. As we shall see, death, too, had his say in binding both men
together, in the odd circumstances of their suicides and in the
arrangements for their burials in far-off Edinburgh. Finally, Hugh
Miller was to make much of the fact that most of his learning came
from the university of life, an instinct that was also very much alive in
Macdonald.

He used it to good effect and one of the characteristics best
remembered by his friends was his undaunted liking for study and
his determination not to be beaten by facts. If they were there to be
learned, Macdonald would commit them to his mind: to get on in life,
to succeed, study was the key and Hector had many doors to open.
As a mature man, though, he was to be predictably ambiguous about
his background and the culture of the crofting folk from which he
sprang. On the one hand he was fiercely proud of his country's
romantic past, of the scenic grandeur of Easter Ross and of the
enduring strengths of the crofting community: on the other, like
many another Victorian Scot who became a leader in the British
imperial scheme of things, he argued for uniformity and a *laissez faire*
cautiousness in political and social matters and in particular he felt
that a standardisation of education could make English the *lingua
franca* of the world empire, all dialects and minority languages having
been banished beyond the reach of civilised man. "It may seem hard
to kill, so to speak, a nation by making another language compulsory,
but it is a sure way and the best," Macdonald was reported as saying
early in 1901 as the Boer War reached its closing stages. "Nothing but
English should be taught, and then the children would think in
English and act as English children."[6]

Hector's pronouncement was the subject of some mild disapproval
in the Highland newspapers but it would have come as little surprise
to those who, like him, had got on in the world. Gaelic was the
language of his childhood and he remained conversant in it until the
end of his life. He became an expert linguist, too, who picked up a
number of other languages, including French, German, Arabic and
Hindi and yet despite those accomplishments, in his public
pronouncements he held rigidly to the belief that there could be no
advancement in the world for his fellow countrymen until they shed
their language and customs and adopted instead the niceties of
English. Macdonald was certainly aware of the contradictions in his
past because when he made the speech about the importance of
English as a means of bringing the Boers within the sphere of British

influence, he ended by drawing an immediate and telling comparison with his native country. When asked whether it would be possible to draw South Africa into the family of Empire, at the conclusion of such a bloody and divisive war, Macdonald replied, "There is the case of the Highlands as a parallel. The almost impossible was done there. I look for the future to education. It is through the young idea that we must succeed in South Africa. English must be the language there."

To prosper, one had to drop the old ways, and in a century that saw the ultimate rise and spread of a British Empire that had to expand in order to survive, many Scots were to leave their homeland and to carve names for themselves as soldiers, administrators, doctors and engineers in far-flung parts of the world: from the Upper Niger to the Straits Settlements, from Hong Kong to the Falkland Islands. To stay at home, to try to achieve something in nineteenth-century Scotland was somehow to court disaster and defeat and so the idea of emigration was a powerful driving force in Scottish life. Macdonald was to spend most of his life abroad in places where social conventions were unimportant, where a meagre salary went farther and where expenses incurred in the line of duty were considerably less. Little wonder, then, that the self-made man who had succeeded, should have turned in later life against the background that had made him. That split in Macdonald's personality, or at least in his intellectual make-up, is important, for having been orphaned from his poor crofting background, with all its contrasting strengths and weaknesses, he was never to be accepted totally by the caste that had adopted him. Certainly, by the time that he had become a major-general and aide-de-camp, Macdonald had moved far and long from the origins of his childhood in the Black Isle.

"We never thought of what we were to be. I supposed I would assist my father on his croft, but Hector never had a liking for the farm and when his brother would be troking about the place, he would be roaming the fields," reported a schoolfriend to a journalist in reply to the question, "What manner of boy was he?". "He always seemed at home with horses. The only thing he expressed a wish for was that he should travel a lot, and many's the time when I went to Dingwall with him I have had to wait while Hector gazed into the shop windows, particularly the newsagent's which was a sort of general store, examining the pictures."[7]

It was Dingwall that claimed him first on the road to those travels to distant parts. The county town of Easter Ross, it stands at the strategic point at the head of the Cromarty Firth where the River Conon flows into the estuary and it had been an important site of Viking settlement in Scotland (it owes its name to a corruption of

Thing Vollr, an early Scandinavian name for the meeting place of parliament; although the town has also used the Gaelic Inverpeffery or Inverferan). Like many other similar Scottish county towns, Dingwall is at first sight somewhat drab and unbecoming, a grey stone place with its buildings huddled along its narrow main street. For the inquisitive, though, close inspection brings its rewards. There is a town house and tolbooth of great antiquity in the High Street and a large nineteenth-century church whose graveyard rings to the names of the great Highland families of the vicinity who rest in the weatherworn burial enclosures: Mackenzie of Fairburn and Strathconon, Murchison of Tarradale, Mackenzie of Cromarty (Easter Ross was also great evangelising country and another possible influence on the young Hector might well have been the memory of the revivalist meetings held by the Rev. John Macdonald, the so-called 'Apostle of the North'. Older people claimed that Macdonald's life at the Battle of Omdurman was held secure through the influence of the 'Apostle', although, as he died in 1849, it is difficult to imagine how powerful that influence might have been.) In the narrow wynds off the main street are some spirited examples of Scottish vernacular architecture and close acquaintance with the town rewards the visitor with its sense of quiet charm.

With little enough to keep him at home, young Hector Macdonald was quick enough to see that the claims of the croft were hardly likely to make his fortune or to help him achieve his ambitions. During the summer months he worked, like the other boys, in the communal activities of the crofting community. Drystane dykes had to be repaired, peat dug in the springtime, cattle tended and fields prepared for harvest, but by the time he was thirteen he had left that all behind and was working as a stable-boy in the employment of A. S. Robertson, the proprietor of the National Hotel in Dingwall. There, no doubt, he would have had his taste for travel whetted by the hotel's many visitors, the majority of whom would have been military officers. The hotel stands in a square at the end of the High Street near the railway station and it had been built originally as a superior government watering hole for civil servants and officers who had cause to spend a night or two in the Easter Ross area while on government duty. Later it became a commercial establishment, losing both the government connection and the temperance that went with it, and to this day it remains the busy focus of social life that it was in Macdonald's day.

Young Hector became a great favourite of the Robertson family and when he pondered his future at the age of fifteen they persuaded him to try his hand at a trade. The local drapery business of Campbell and

and Mackenzie in the High Street had an opening for a smart boy and in the summer of 1868 Macdonald was engaged by them as an apprentice draper. For the next two years he was to work in an institutionalised world which was run like a workhouse but which cultivated the appearance of servile gentility.

3

Off for a soldier

Within a year Hector had begun to tire of selling yard after yard of blue serge to visiting Highlanders and so his parents and the Robertsons, fearful that the headstrong boy might take matters into his own hands, arranged a further term of apprenticeship in nearby Inverness, a larger town than Dingwall, offering more pleasures and well away from the apron strings at home. Perhaps the boy would learn that standing on his two feet took up time enough to keep him free of idle temptations. There, he entered the employment of the Royal Clan and Tartan Warehouse, a curious Gothic building which also housed the Inverness Y.M.C.A. and which stood at the corner of the High Street with Castle Street.

Then, as now, Inverness was a busy, bustling town, the "Capital of the Highlands", with its rail-head and cattle-market, its castle and cathedral. Following the arrival of the railway to the Highlands it was well on its way to becoming a tourist mecca. It was also the town nearest to the massive eighteenth-century garrison of Fort George which juts stoically into the chill waters of the Moray Firth at the village of Ardersier. Built in 1748 during the bitter years that followed the failure of the '45 Jacobite rebellion, it proclaims its purpose in its enormous defensive walls and barrack blocks to house some two thousand men: to provide a significant military establishment and presence in a locality that had been prone in recent years to take up arms against the government and the Hanoverian succession. Gradually it became the centre of military affairs in the Highlands and its name is forever linked with the names of two regiments which recruited from the locality—the Cameron Highlanders and the Seaforth Highlanders (amalgamated in 1961 to form the present-day Queen's Own Highlanders). Although it lies ten miles east of Inverness, soldiers from the garrison were constant visitors to the town to sample its drink, dance halls and women while on short leave passes. Inverness may not have been a garrison town but it was recognised by the army as being a principal centre for recruitment into the Highland regiments.

Unlike many other shopkeepers of his day, William Mackay, the owner of the Royal Clan and Tartan Warehouse, was a humane employer. His apprentices were not obliged to "live in" as were their counterparts in many another large city in Britain; in a place like Inverness which closed its doors early in the evening and opened them again at a reasonable hour of morning, the working hours were liberal enough and although Hector had to sign an indentation of apprenticeship with Mr Mackay, his leisure hours were more or less his own. Under the terms of his agreement he promised to obey his employer, to keep shop hours, to dress neatly and to behave with decorum in private and in public.

> Young men must dress as respectably as when engaged—black coats and vests. Young men must not stand behind the counter (after closing excepted) or speak to customers with their coats off—fine 6d. Young ladies must wear black dresses made to clear the ground (showroom young ladies excepted), white linen collars and cuffs, and the hair arranged in a neat and becoming manner.[1]

Those are shop rules of a London silk warehouse of the same period but with their black-dressed stuffiness and white-collared stiffness they offer chill evidence about what it was like to enter the hard-edged commercial world of the Victorian shopkeeper. For a strapping crofter's son used to an open air life it must have been a restricting and unfriendly ambience to which he found himself translated. Besides, another aspect of the job may not have appealed to his independent spirit: in effect, the rules ensured that the apprentice draper of the eighteen-sixties was engaged to learn not so much about the niceties of napery or how many yards made a skirt length; rather they were becoming salesmen who had to learn the vital techniques of enticing would-be shoppers to make a purchase.

With time hanging heavy on his hands and with his requests for a post as a commercial traveller falling on stony ground, Hector Macdonald turned for solace to the pleasures of a volunteer. Shortly after arriving in Inverness he joined the Merchants' Company of the Inverness Highland Rifle Volunteers which was attached to the 1st Battalion of the Cameron Highlanders. The militia had long been considered to be a well-stocked larder for recruiting to the regular regiments of the British army and under the Cardwell army reforms of 1871 local militia or volunteer units were linked to regiments of the line. Thus it was to be expected that many of the rifle volunteers would find their way into the ranks of the Cameron Highlanders. Localisation, it was hoped, would lead to pride in a regiment's achievements and the army would be ensured a steady supply of reasonably trained, well-turned out recruits who were keen on the army as a career, instead of having to rely on the brutal and heavy-handed method of press-ganging the unemployed into becoming regimental cannon-fodder. It was a sensible, workmanlike policy and light years removed from that which had been in force only twenty years before.

> The Militia would be drawn up in line, and the officers, or non-commissioned officers, from the regiments requiring volunteers, would give a glowing description of their several regiments, describing the victories they had gained, and the honours they had acquired, and concluded by offering a bounty, to volunteers for life £14, to volunteers for the limited period of seven years £11. If these inducements were not effectual in getting men, then coercive methods were adopted; heavy and long field exercises were forced on them, which were so oppressive that to escape them men would embrace the alternative and join the colours.[2]

The members of the Inverness Highland Rifle Volunteers were expected to drill regularly and to attend rifle practice on the butts but by 1870, with talk of war in Europe on everyone's lips, the enthusiasm was so great that Macdonald's company would rise at six o'clock in the morning to get in two hours of daily drilling before the day's work began in earnest. Their commander was a hoary veteran of Lucknow and the Indian Mutiny called Sergeant-Major Pocock and he was to exert a strong influence on Macdonald. Precision drilling was his *forte*: it was an important part of any soldier's training and in an army that still relied on moving large numbers of men in close formation in the field it could frequently mean the difference between life and death. It was also intended to turn men into automatons who could be trusted to hold their positions and to respond to orders in a trustworthy, calm and obedient way. The intricacies of the army regulation drillbook fascinated Macdonald and from that early age he acclimatised himself both to the symmetry of formal drill movements and also to the ways in which they could be used to move men safely and effectively during the confusion of battle.

He threw himself into the militia with enthusiasm, and, later, his companions were to remember his pride in his uniform and his confident upright stance: the militia records reveal that he was 5 feet 8½ inches in height, dark-haired and spare of build. With his later training he was to become noticed for the breadth of his shoulders and for the taut muscularity of his stocky frame. People with army connections became his constant companions. His lodgings were shared with an ex-sergeant and he encouraged Hector with bouts of extra drilling and tales of army lore—and on one famous occasion both were almost thrown out of the house by an angry landlady who discovered the sergeant busy teaching his recruit bayonet drill with a new set of pillows and a broomstick!

Another acquaintance amongst the volunteers was Piper A. E. Findlater, also destined for the Gordons, who was to win a Victoria Cross and immortal renown for the part he played in the storming of the Dargai heights in 1897. His part in that heroic action won Findlater universal acclaim—he continued to play the Gordon's regimental march 'Cock of the North' to rally the men, despite being shot through both ankles and taking scant cover behind the rocks—and he became a national hero when the regiment returned to Britain. As the regimental history coyly records: " . . . the Scotsmen in London would have let him swim in champagne, and the daily cheers of the multitude were enough to turn an older head than that on this young shoulder". The action, which took place in the north-west frontier was also made famous by the words of the Gordon's Colonel Mathias when his battalion was ordered to advance in the murderous Afridi fire: "The General says this hill must be taken at all costs—the Gordon Highlanders will take it."[3]

At home in Rootfield the news that Hector was army-mad was met with little enthusiasm and the fears were justified when he arrived home for a short holiday in the winter of 1869. Instead of throwing himself into the activities of the croft or spending time with his old friends, Macdonald spent most of his holiday teaching the boys of the Mulbuie school how to drill. He had also become friendly with an Inverness lad who had just finished his training with the Royal Engineers at Chatham. To the Rootfield family the signs were ominous: it looked as if Hector was about to go for a soldier.

Such a thing was frowned upon in a quiet God-fearing community as Mulbuie was. Only riff-raff of the worst sort joined the army and the figure of the kilted, bewhiskered recruiting sergeant was a spectre that haunted country areas only when the harvests failed or the winters were bitter. Jack Frost, it was said, continued to be the British army's most successful recruiter of men. Memories were strong, too, of the injustices and horrors of the Crimean War of 1855 and 1856, and as the government only required a limited number of soldiers on garrison duty in Britain, most soldiering was done within the Empire, and that meant far-off India. There, the rank and file of the British army were supposed to carry out the necessary protection and maintainace of the Empire while people safely tucked at home in bed in Britain refused to give Tommy more than a moment's thought.

For it's Tommy this, an' Tommy that, an' "Chuck him out, the brute!"
But it's "Saviour of 'is country" when the guns begin to shoot;
An' it's Tommy this, an' Tommy that, an' anything you please;
An' Tommy ain't a bloomin' fool—you bet that Tommy sees!

Throughout the winter and spring of 1870 Macdonald brooded on
whether or not to follow in the footsteps of Kipling's "Tommy", and
all the while the fire generated by the Franco-Prussian hostilities
gripped the streets of Inverness. Recruiting sergeants stood at street
corners biding their time, waiting for the likeliest looking recruits. On
the 11th June 1870, after a lengthy discussion with his Engineer
friend, Macdonald did what his parents and friends always suspected
he would one day do. He walked up to a sergeant of the 92nd
Highlanders and said that he wanted to enlist. As we have seen, he
lied a little about his age, but he was strong, clean and enthusiastic,
an ideal recruit for a line regiment of the British army.

The sergeant marched him to a small public house in Castle Street,
known as the Old Peahen, and today long since disappeared beneath
the bulk of the town hall. There he was offered the traditional dram,
presented with the Queens' shilling and signed up as a private
soldier in the army of Queen Victoria. "I never regretted that action,"
Madonald said in a public speech after the successful Sudan campaign of 1898. "As I shook hands with the man who enlisted me, I
made up my mind to do my best and make a name for myself in the
army."[4]

That prediction was to come true, but by promising to serve his
Queen and his country unto death, Macdonald had also broken the
conditions of his indenture to William Mackay of the Royal Clan and
Tartan Warehouse. When his apprentice failed to turn up the
following day, Mackay was more than a little annoyed to hear from
his staff that Macdonald had last been seen marching off with a
recruiting sergeant. All the virtues of small town morality had been
offended. Not only had he thrown up a good job for a place in a
group of common ruffians, but he done it by stealth and without
serving his time! It took several years for Macdonald to contact his
old employer and that was only to be when he had gained his
commission and had started to rise in the world. In a tongue-in-cheek
sort of way he paid his compliments to his early training in the
warehouse, acknowledging that "any strides I made in my profession,
or any more I may make, are due, in a marked measure, to
observance and imitation (so far as could be applied to a soldier's
life) of your methodical and business-like manner of conducting your
establishment; for I may add that what you taught—punctuality,
order, cleanliness, method, and (here I fell with you and received a

lesson) implicit faith and obedience—are the main attributes of a good soldier." And he ended the letter by offering a small piece of practical advice: " . . . never let your employees lodge with soldiers or with those who were soldiers for as sure as you do you may look out to losing some of them".[5]

At home the information was met with dismay, and Mrs Macdonald might well have echoed the sentiments of another mother, Mrs Robertson in distant Lincolnshire whose son William also joined up and, like Macdonald, was destined to rise through the ranks to become a high-ranking officer (Field-Marshal Sir William Robertson): "There are plenty of things Steady Young Men can do when they can read and write as you can . . . the army is a refuge for all Idle People . . . I shall name it to no one for I am ashamed to think of it. I would rather Bury you than see you in a red coat."[6]

A forthright and heartfelt statement of that kind was in stark contrast to the newspapers' adulation of both men in later life and after the Boer War when Macdonald was a national hero, jingoism had it that a soldier's life was better than remaining in the unmanly ambience of a draper's shop: " . . . the mixed blood that ran in Hector Macdonald's veins made him, like young Norval, rebel against every calling but the career of arms and prompted him to exchange the yard measure of an effeminate counter-jumper for the musket of a son of Mars".

The society that Macdonald joined after he was taken from Inverness to Fort George had a peculiarly family atmosphere. Even before the Cardwell reforms Scottish regiments had drawn heavily on traditional recruiting grounds. The Camerons and Seaforths recruited mainly from the northern counties and had not a detachment of Gordons been at Fort George Macdonald would have probably joined the Camerons. There was a strong historical tradition of militarism in Scotland and many soldiers in the Highland regiments looked on themselves as continuing the traditions of their forebears, mercenaries who had fought in the Scots Brigades of the crowns of France, Italy, the German states and Sweden. Despite official social disapproval of the army in Scotland, it was not too bad a life. Soldiers in Highland regiments (and many were English and Irish men) were usually well-fed, decently clad and reasonably literate. "It was the writing, quite as much as the fighting, of the Scottish regiments that distinguished them," wrote Thomas Somerville in his *Autobiography of a Working Man.*

Twenty-seven Scottish regiments had been raised on the orders of William Pitt after the '45 rebellion, both as a means of channelling traditional Scottish aggression into the military service of Empire and, more slyly perhaps, to provide a focus for national inspiration. With

their modified military kilts and trappings, and pipe and drum bands
with martial melodies the Highland regiments made a proud sight;
and in a country bereft of an identity they made a good and colourful
substitute. Better still, they could also be used to the country's and to
the Empire's best advantage. Given so much romance it was little
wonder that they attracted to them the most potent myths of Scottish
prowess of arms.

Hardly a nineteenth-century campaign passed but that the Scots
personified themselves as the epitome of aggression and fighting
skill: the charge of the Gordons with the Scots Greys at Waterloo, the
Thin Red line of the 93rd Highlanders at Balaclava, Sir Colin
Campbell and the Highland Brigade at Lucknow; wherever the
British army fought, the Scots were always well to the fore. In tandem
a legend also grew up that Scots bravery and personal courage had to
compensate for English inefficiency or cowardice. (Thus at
Magersfontein, during the Boer War, the crushing defeat of the
Highland Brigade was put down to incompetence and the jealousy of
the predominantly English general staff, and the belief grew in
Scotland that the brigade would not have been sacrificed had it not
come from north of Potters Bar.) Those were heady beliefs and
prejudices, powerful enough to fuel the instinct for traditions in
Scotland, so that the Scottish soldier, although he might have been
dismissed as a pariah at close quarters, was nevertheless a powerful
embodiment of nationhood and leading Scottish generals were very
important figures indeed.

The Gordons—the 92nd Highlanders—had a reputation second to
none as one of the most fiercesome cutting edges of the British army.
They also enjoyed a name for being good-natured and open-handed,
and although it was a strict regiment that Macdonald encountered
when he joined up, it was also a friendly welcoming one. From Fort
George he went by train to Aberdeen where a sergeant met him and
took him to the Castle Hill barracks where he was to learn his basic
training. Pipe-Major George Stuart, who enlisted with Macdonald,
remembered his "fine soldier-like bearing with his broad shoulders
and full chest. His dark hair and moustache, and his general
expression of countenance emphasised his splendid physique and he
struck you at once as a soldier born." There were other hallmarks that
singled him out. He kept away from the canteen and wasn't the one
for the pewter or the pipe. "He generally occupied his spare time in
studying and it is a fact that he enlisted with a drill book in his
pocket. Study, study, study was the keynote of his life, and promotion
was the ambition ever in his head."[7]

It would have been a dull set of officers who had not recognised

Macdonald's attainments and at the end of his period of initial training he was promoted lance-corporal and allowed a few days leave to visit his parents at Rootfield, prior to his company's embarkation to join the regiment at Jullundur in northern India. He left in January 1871 with a draft of eighty-six non-commissioned officers and men under the command of Lieutenant D.F. Gordon as replacements for invalids and time-expired men being given the opportunity to return home, and the troopship's route took them from Portsmouth through the newly-opened Suez Canal to land at Bombay where they rested at the famous transit camp at Deolali before making the long journey north.

During the long voyage, Macdonald and another recruit, John Robertson, were made "salt water corporals", an honorary rank given to soldiers placed in responsible positions while at sea, and usually relinquished when the ship reached port. However, when the draft arrived at the regiment's headquarters, Lieutenant Gordon recommended to the colonel, Forbes Macbean, that both men be allowed to keep their new ranks. A hurried consultation took place with the sergeant-major who wanted to check the men's ability to drill, and Macdonald had taken another step on the road to promotion. Two stripes were sewn onto his white linen uniform jacket (the 92nd's uniform in India, together with the kilt and white helmet) and Macdonald entered 'C' company which was under the command of Captain Harry Brooke, the son of an Aberdeenshire landowner.

Macdonald's regiment had been in India since March 1868, stationed at Jullundur, near Amritsar in northern India, on garrison duty. Life in the cantonment was, on the whole, tolerable and comfortable. The barracks were large and airy, there was a library and a theatre, a games room with billiards and bagetelle tables, and the food was fresh and plentiful. Only malaria and dysentry were problems and convalescing soldiers were sent to the cooler and fresher air of Dalhousie in the nearby Chumba Hills. Discipline was relaxed, too, and by the year of the 92nd's arrival in India corporal punishment had been abolished in the British army except as a last resort on active service. It disappeared finally in 1881 and so passed into history one of the most degrading and dehumanising customs in Britain's army. Punishments of up to two hundred lashes had not been uncommon and it was used, regularly, for the pettiest of offences: inefficient officers were happy to see its employment to cover up their own shortcomings. With the British system of keeping most of its standing army abroad, India had had its fair share of that kind of officer, men who had purchased their commissions and who tended to take their status and their pleasures seriously, their professional duties less so. Fox hunting, polo and gambling had been the real pastimes of a gentleman: parade ground drill an onerous bore.

The 92nd had been better served than most other regiments on that score but in the past they, too, would have possessed a handful of gentlemen officers who had been happy to devolve responsibility onto the capable shoulders of the non-commissioned officers. However, by 1871 all that had begun to change. The Cardwell reforms had abolished the purchase of commissions, a system that had previously caused much aggravation and no little ineffeciency within the army. Until 1871, officers had been able to purchase their commissions up to the rank of lieutenant-colonel—a lump sum was paid on the first commission and additional sums on each promotion. So officers came only from the monied classes and were supposed to have healthy private incomes. "Good God," a young subaltern is supposed to have said on hearing that the War Office had deposited £100 in his bank account. "Do they actually pay us?"

Only those with inherited wealth became officers in the better regiments, irrespective of their ability or intelligence, and the system had also led to the abuses of young officers offering cash inducements to older men to retire earlier. Although Cardwell's changes were not wholly welcomed by everyone—the 92nd's regimental history described the reforms as "a boon to the officers, but a great cost to the country"—they did ensure greater efficiency and they also presented the first opportunity for rankers to gain commissions through merit. When Macdonald arrived in India, it was then possible for a private to become an officer, if he showed a disposition to make his way in the army.

4

A Gay and Gallant Gordon

The regiment that Macdonald had joined, the 92nd, or Gordon, Highlanders, had been raised in 1794 by the 4th Duke of Gordon. Tradition had it that it has been "kissed into being", the story told that Jean, the duke's beautiful wife, accompanied her husband on his recruiting expeditions into the north-east homelands so that she could offer a kiss to every man who joined the colours. As an added inducement the King's shilling was held between her lips and it was not long before three regiments had been raised by this powerful family which had remained loyal to the Hanoverian succession during the '45. Eventually they were formed into one regiment, the 100th, under the command of the Duke's son, the Marquis of Huntly, but within five years they had been renumbered the 92nd. (It is a measure of Britain's military conservatism that the system of numbering regiments which Wellington used at Waterloo continued well into the century.)

They quickly gained a reputation as a proud fighting force and a glimpse at their battle honours shows that hardly a year passed from their formation but that they were not in action somewhere. In 1799 they cut their teeth at Egmont-op-zee when they took the brunt of a vicious charge by six thousand French troops and by keeping good order in the face of fierce hand-to-hand fighting they preserved the British lines and helped to win the day. In the Peninsular War they fought in every battle and after the death of Sir John Moore at Corunna they adopted the use of black buttons in their spats in perpetual mourning for a general they had tried their best to protect—and the tradition is still preserved in the Gordons uniform of today. It was at Waterloo, though, that they earned their greatest renown. At a critical moment in the battle the heavy cavalry charged the French lines and as the Royal Scots Greys advanced into the attack the men of the Gordons clung impetuously onto the troopers' stirrups to charge into battle with the cry of "Scotland for ever!" Ever since that heroic feat of arms the two regiments (the Royal Scots

Greys are now the Royal Scots Dragoon Guards following their amalgamation with the 3rd Carabiniers) have enjoyed close and friendly links. Until 1872 when they adopted the stag's head cap badge of the Gordon family, with the motto "Bydand" (meaning steadfast or enduring), their cap badge was the Sphinx, with the motto "Egypt" in honour of their role in the army operations in that country in 1800 during the war with France. It was with good reason that their nickname was "The Gay and Gallant Gordons".

When in India—and they had seen active service there, on and off, since the middle of the century—the 92nd were part of an army of fifty-two British battalions on constant active service in the sub-continent. Official policy since the Mutiny decreed that there should always be one British soldier for every two sepoys and the duty of the British soldier was to maintain the *Pax Britannica* and to take part in the subjugation of reluctant subject people like the troublesome tribes of the North-West Frontier. Queen Victoria had herself set the mood for the preservation of her Empire in her private writings: "If we are to *maintain* our position as a *first-rate* Power, we must, with our Indian Empire and large Colonies, be *Prepared* for *attacks* and *wars, somewhere* or *other* CONTINUALLY." That she was correct in her assessment can be seen in the plain facts of history. Between 1837 and 1901, the long era of Victoria's reign, not a single year passed without British soldiers being in action somewhere, fighting what Kipling called "the savage wars of peace" and what were more aptly known as Queen Victoria's little wars of Empire. Those little wars— rebellions, mutinies, local uprisings—posed no real threat to the fabric of Empire and much of the fighting in the remoter parts of the world was simply an excuse to exercise power or to prevent other empires, such as the French or Russian, from exercising theirs. And as Hilaire Belloc noted, victories against badly equipped native armies armed with obselete and in many cases medieval weapons, were hardly the stuff of heroism.

> Whatever happens we have got
> The Maxim gun and they have not.

To fight those battles Britain had an army composed largely of volunteers, which was small, unprofessional and immobile by contemporary European standards, though most of its soldiers were brave to a man. It recruited its officer corps from the ranks of the landed gentry and its other ranks came from the army of the unemployed or unemployable. Strategic planning was unheard of, most regulations were based on eighteenth-century principles and in the smarter regiments there was an active discrimination against intelligent officers who took an interest in the mechanics or the theories of their chosen profession. "Brains. I don't beliveve in brains," said the Duke of Cambridge, commander-in-chief of the British army in 1895 to a fellow staff officer. "You haven't any, I know, sir."[1] Cambridge, the cousin of Queen Victoria, held his position for forty years and not only did he oppose change in the army but also quarrelled bitterly with anyone who proposed it. Such was the speed of thinking in the British army of the last two decades of the nineteenth century that combat theories were still based on the slow, inexorable movement forward of troops in tight formation which had won the day at the Battle of Fontenoy in 1745.

The antidote was precision drilling and at that the British army excelled. In any good foot regiment the drill corporal was king and Macdonald, remembering his early schooling in the volunteers made it his own, putting the men of 'C' company through the endless variety of exercises from the army drillbook until they could be done blindfolded. Later, as an officer, Macdonald was to serve on a War Office committee which had been established to review drilling procedures in the British army, and although by then he had been won over by the tactics of rapid deployment of troops armed with high velocity weapons as used in the American Civil War and in the Franco-Prussian War, he never lost his belief in the disciplinary aspects of drilling.

Route marches were the other means of training and of instilling a sense of *cameraderie* within a regiment. In a country as large as India they were a necessary evil too, and the movement of regiments was largely governed by their ability to shift quickly over the long and dusty roads between cantonments.

> The dairy, bakery, cooks and camp-followers moved off each evening twelve hours in advance of the Battalion, so that rations could be drawn and breakfast ready by the time the Battalion arrived. There was no breakfast before we started out on our march, which on some days was stiffer than others, but any man who chose to do so could give his name to the Colour Sergeant who would put it down on the list of men who would be daily supplied with a good meat sandwich and a pint of tea at the coffee-halt for which two annas a day was deducted from their pay. The Battalion coffee-bar supplied the sandwiches and tea, which were issued out after half the day's march had been completed. We always knew when we were approaching the coffee-halt, where we had half an hour's rest by the drums striking up with the tune of *Polly put the kettle on and we'll all have tea.*[2]

That description of the arrangements made for the route march of the
Royal Welch Fusiliers to Chakrata by Frank Richards in his memoirs,
Old Soldier Sahib, could have been echoed by any old sweat who had
done his time in India in the period up to the beginning of the First
World War.

The same route to Chakrata was taken by the 92nd in March 1872
and they were to stay there until 22nd November 1873 when they set
off on the 495-mile march to Multan. They reached there on 13th
January 1874. It was to be the regiment's home for the next two years
and it was during this period that Corporal Macdonald was raised to
the olympian heights of colour-sergeant. The promotion was made by
the colonel, A.W. Cameron, who had succeeded Forbes Macbean in
December 1873. The son of Cameron of Lochailort, he was a Gaelic
speaker who prided himself on his quiet knowledge of the Highland
way of life and he was very popular with his men. Macdonald said
later that when Cameron sent for him, he said, "Corporal Macdonald,
there is a vacancy for a sergeant, and though you are a young soldier,
I intend to make you, but I would have you remember that a sergeant
in the Gordon Highlanders is equal to a member of parliament and I
expect you to behave accordingly!" The bemused corporal asked the
sergeant-major what the colonel had implied and received the
answer, "Oh, my lad, he only means that he respects us, and he wants
us to respect ourselves."[3] The promotion gave Macdonald access to
the élite corps of the non-commissioned officers and the command of
'C' company, his pay was increased and more importantly for him he
won the respect of his fellow men—for a soldier still in his twenties
he had come a long way.

On the 13th January 1876 a detachment of the Gordons was sent
by rail to Lahore on the occasion of the visit of the Prince of Wales to
India. A guard of honour of one hundred men plus the drums and
pipes of the regiment camped out in the grounds of Government
House and to Macdonald fell the honour of commanding the sentry
detail outside the tent of the man who was to become King Edward
VII. At the height of Macdonald's fame, the incident was remembered
with much amusement by both parties. There are several versions of
the story but the most likely one, given the regiment's movements in
1876 was published in the *Daily Chronicle* following Macdonald's
audition with the Prince of Wales at Marlborough House. "The Prince
asked Fighting Mac how it was that they had not met before. 'Pardon
me, sir, I think we have,' was the reply. 'Where can that have been?'
asked the Prince, surprised. 'When you were in India, sir, I did
sentry-go outside your tent.' 'But why was a sentry needed outside
my tent?' The answer, which need not be repeated here, caused His

Royal Highness considerable amusement but when he had regained
control of his features, he held out his hand and said, 'General
Macdonald, you were doing sentry-go in 1876 and now you are a
general in the British army. I am proud to have met you.' "

Later that same year, 1876, the regiment was again involved in
ceremonial duties when it took part in the great durbar to proclaim
Queen Victoria Empress of India. It was a glittering occasion with
the princes of India vying one with another to express their loyalty to
the Empress in terms of the magnificence of their trappings and the
numbers in their retinues. Set against them were the troops of the
British army in India—kilted Highlanders, smart blue-coated lancers,
the red tunics of the English county regiments—and behind them
the regiments of the Indian Army: the dark green uniforms and blue
and white puggrees of the Bombay Cavalry, the varied hues of the
Punjab, Sikh and Pathan regiments, and the dash and *élan* of the
native cavalry with famous names like Hodson's Horse and the
Guides from the North-West Frontier Province. After the celebrations, which seem to have been a hybrid cross between the best of
the ancient ceremonials of Britain and India, the Gordons returned to
Multan before moving off to Sitapur in February 1877 when they
exchanged their Snider rifles for the newer Martini-Henry high
velocity breech-loading rifle.

They stayed in the Sitapur cantonment until December 1878 when
they began the march up to the North-West Frontier as the drums of
war began to beat again in that troubled area of the Empire. Their
first stop was Kohat where they met, for the first time, the
commander of the army they were about to join, a little known Indian
Army officer called General Frederick Sleigh Roberts (later to
become Field-Marshal Lord Roberts of Kandahar, Chief of the
Imperial General Staff). He was much impressed by what he found.
"Towards the end of 1879 I paid a visit to Kohat and had the pleasure
of welcoming to the province that grand regiment, the 92nd
Highlanders, which had been sent up in readiness to join my column
in the event of an advance on Kabul becoming necessary."[4]

To discover the origins of why a march to Kabul in distant
Afghanistan should have become neccessary we have to go back to
1839. Then, at a time when Britain was consolidating its power in
India, the administrators began to fear that Russia or Persia might
seek to infiltrate the Raj through the North-West Frontier by gaining
a sphere of influence in Afghanistan, an independent buffer state
between the Russian and the British empires. Dost Muhammad, the
Amir of Afghanistan was tolerably friendly towards the British but
that was not enough for the Governor-General of India, Lord

Auckland, who decided that his north-western flank would be safer if a British puppet—in this case the weak and despotic Shah Shuja—were on the throne. The coup, with British military support, succeeded, but the fiery Afghans refused to bow to the British administration and events came to a head in January 1842 when the retreating British—men, women and children—were cut to pieces in the mountain passes, only one man, Dr William Brydon, surviving, and then only because the thickness of a copy of *Blackwood's Magazine* stuffed into his topee saved his head from an Afghan swordstroke. Of course, the British restored their "pride" when General George Pollock marched up to Kabul and burned down the Great Bazaar. But the British had not learned the lesson of keeping their noses out of Afghanistan's affairs, and skirmishes and little wars were to break out along the frontier for the rest of the century.

The trouble started again during the eighteen-sixties when a series of Russian annexations of neighbouring Tashkent, Samarkand and Khiva made the British in India fear that their rivals were attempting a pincer movement on the sub-continent. Events reached a culmination in 1877 when the Amir, Shere Ali, the third son of the deposed Dost Muhammad, entertained a Russian delegation but refused to allow a British mission to enter his country. His decision was a severe blow to national pride and the British agreed that if Shere Ali had chosen not to invite a British presence in his country, then, like it or not, he would jolly well have to make do with one. Accordingly, a British column set off from Peshawar for the frontier only to be repulsed when it reached the border. In Britain's outraged eyes there was nothing for it but to raise an army and invade Afghanistan just to show the Amir who really controlled the sub-continent. Three field forces were raised—the first, the Peshawar Valley Field Force, under the command of Lieutenant-General Sam Browne (the eponymous designer of the belt) which would advance on the Khyber Pass; the second, the Kandahar Field Force, under Major-General Donald Stewart and, finally, the Kurram Valley Field Force, a supposedly inferior army made up largely of native troops under General Roberts.

Roberts entered Afghanistan in November 1878 and held the Kurram Valley but ahead of him lay a mountainous defile, Peiwar Kotal, which the Afghans had made into a well-nigh impregnable position. What followed made Roberts' name. He directed his best troops, including the 5th Gurkhas and a detachment of Seaforth Highlanders, on a night march around the left hand side of the mountain and surrounded the astonished Afghans. With the success of the other two armies the invasion was a victory in military terms; a treaty was signed with Yakub Khan, the new Amir, at Gandamuk and Roberts was left to consolidate the frontier in the Kurram Valley. Flushed with success he asked for, and received, reinforcements, in the shape of cavalry and artillery, and in his opinion best of all, the 92nd Gordon Highlanders.

5

Officer and Gentleman

It was not long before Roberts was in action again. By the Treaty of Gandamuk the Kurram Valley was ceded to Britain by way of reparation and Yakub Khan agreed to the proposal that a British mission should be allowed to set up residence in Kabul. Thinking that the emergency was over, the government in India dispersed Browne's and Stewart's field forces, leaving only Roberts' army in the Kurram Valley. The Gordons were ordered to proceed up to the frontier at Alikhel and arrangements were made in July 1879 for the transport to Kabul of the British emissary and plenipotentiary, Pierre Louis Napoleon Cavagnari. He was an odd choice for the post: the son of the marriage of one of Napoleon's generals to the daughter of an old Anglo-Irish family, he had fought with distinction in the Indian Mutiny and had received rapid promotion afterwards in the Indian political service.

Roberts distrusted Cavagnari and, more importantly, feared for his safety in Kabul. At the final dinner before the mission set off he could not bring himself to toast its success, and like many another Empire builder he was firmly of the opinion that the treaty had been signed before "we had instilled that awe of us into the Afghan nation which would have been the only reliable guarantee for the safety of the Mission".[1] Even if those uncompromising words had been the right policy it would have been extremely difficult to have put Roberts' words into action. The terrain of the frontier was rocky and mountainous, the roads narrow and twisting into steep valleys tailor-made for ambush, and the local tribes owed allegiance to no one except to those in the immediate surrounding territory. Furthermore, successive Amirs had been forced to bribe tribes like the Ghilzais to allow the free passage of people and merchandise along the border roads. As other would-be invaders have discovered, Afghanistan is a notoriously difficult country for an invading power to police—just as the Russians have been saved on many occasions by the intervention of General Winter, so it seemed had the Afghans relied on the services of Colonel Mountain.

Despite their gun-boatish tang, Roberts' words were in the end justified. At the beginning of September the message came through from Kabul that Cavagnari and his staff had been slaughtered to a man. A disenchanted government in Simla ordered Roberts to return immediately to the frontier and to take steps to instil "that awe of us" into the Afghans and to punish them accordingly. Roberts was on the point of returning home for a well-deserved furlough and it took him three weeks to organise the necessary reinforcements and transport for his expedition. A Kabul Field Force was formed and the Gordons were placed in the First Infantry Brigade under the command of Brigadier-General Herbert Macpherson, V.C. and ordered to guard the Shutargardan Pass at the village of Kushi.

There they set about deploying themselves for the coming fight. Under the command of Captain MacCallum and Lieutenant Grant, a hundred men, including those of Hector Macdonald's 'C' company, were sent up to occupy the fort at Karatiga which afforded a splendid view of the mountainous pass and good sightlines over the surrounding countryside. The scene that met the Gordons there was nightmarish. Dead camels littered the landscape and the stench from the rotting carcases was so overpowering that several soldiers had to be sent back to base, physically sickened by the horrid experience. But, whatever the inconveniences of finding themselves in an animals' graveyard, the fort at Karatiga gave MacCallum and his men an important vantage point. On the evening of the 27th September he noticed the deployment of some two thousand Afghans who were obviously taking up position to ambush Roberts and his advance column of cavalry made up of units from the 9th Lancers and the 5th Punjab Cavalry. Lieutenant Grant was sent with a detachment of twenty-five men to warn Roberts and they arrived not a moment too soon. The column was on the point of entering the pass and the message had just been handed over when Roberts and his party came under heavy fire from the tribesmen hidden in the rocks above them. Roberts survived, but his medical officer, Dr Townsend was badly injured and several Punjabi cavalrymen were killed.

The exact location of the ambush was known as the Hazar Darakht defile (or the Pass of a Thousand Trees) and it was there that Macdonald's hour came. He had been sent from Karatiga onto the surrounding hillside with a party of eighteen Gordons and forty-five men from the 3rd Sikhs under the command of a native non-commissioned officer (jemadar) Sher Mahommed Khan. As their comrades in the valley below attempted to sweep the enemy back towards the main body of the army, it soon became obvious to

Macdonald that the Afghans held a well-nigh impregnable position in the precipitious hills and that any attack from below would spell disaster for his ill-prepared comrades under Lieutenant Grant. Macdonald took command, rallied the Sikhs to him and summed up the position. A full frontal attack was madness and so the only solution was to take away from the Afghans their advantage of superior cover. Quickly and resolutely, he led his men across a tumbling stream that ran through the rocky defile, to take cover on the opposite side where lay the hidden enemy. Then they made their way up the hillside until they were above the Afghans.

It was a brave move and one that called for cool-headed daring: the men were under continuous fire and, unused to being in action as they were, the clatter and riccochet of bullets from a hidden enemy must have been an unnerving experience, especially as each man would have known that the British force was vastly outnumbered. When the Afghans did attack Macdonald kept to the drillbook. He waited until they were within three hundred yards and then gave the order for rapid controlled fire into the advancing Afghans who, having no taste for being at the receiving end of tactics usually employed by their leaders, quickly withdrew. Macdonald's leadership required not only conspicuous personal heroism but also a sense of command and his star saw to it that it was carried out under the knowing eyes of his commander, General Roberts.

For his bravery Macdonald was mentioned in the dispatches of the 15th October:

> Meanwhile a warm engagement had for some hours been carried on in the direction of Karatiga, and presently large numbers of the enemy were seen retreating before a small detachment of the 92nd Highlanders and the 3rd Sikhs, which had been sent out from Karatiga, and which were, with excellent judgement and boldness, led up a steep spur commanding the defile. The energy and skill with which this party was handled reflected the highest credit on Colour-Sergeant Hector Macdonald, 92nd Highlanders, and Jemadar Sher Mahommed, 3rd Sikhs. But for their excellent services on this occasion, it might probably have been impossible to carry out the programme of our march.[2]

As it was, Roberts was able to pass through the Shutargardan Pass and to reach the village of Kushi where he had arranged to meet the Amir, Yakub Khan. As the small victorious force of Gordons returned to Karatiga, records the regimental history, a comrade of Macdonald's shouted out to him, "We'll mak' ye an officer for this day's work, sergeant!" "Aye," cried another, "and a General too!"[3] As the regiment's historian, Lieutenant-Colonel Greenhill Gardyne recorded generously in the same account, they were to be prophetic words.

Although the first battle had been won, the war was far from over and it was Roberts' responsibility to discover from the Amir the identity of the murderers and also what steps had been taken to guarantee the safety of the British mission. Yakub Khan denied all knowledge of the event and his expressions of grief and regret only served to anger further the British commander who was not over-impressed by his Afghan adversary. "He was an insignificant-looking man, about thirty-two years of age, with a receding forehead, a conical-shaped head, and no chin to speak of, and he gave me the idea of being entirely wanting in that force of character without which no one could hope to govern or hold in check the warlike and turbulent people of Afghanistan."[4]

In the end Roberts realised that he was being stalled and so he set off for Kabul to carry out the retribution that was the purpose of his expedition. On the route he encountered little in the way of opposition until he reached the small village of Charasiah which lay ten miles to the south-west of the city. There, on the high hills which rose all around the cultivated fields and the attractive orchards belonging to the villagers, the Afghan army and units of irregular tribesmen had taken up their positions and threatened to attack the British force while it was still on the march. Part of the problem facing Roberts was the occupation of a gorge on the River Logar, called Sang-i-nawishta, which carried the road to the village and which could be used by the enemy as their main channel of attack, or, if it became necessary, of retreat. Because it was impossible to deploy the mountain guns of the Royal Horse Artillery, Roberts ordered the gorge to be cleared by the infantry and that duty fell to an officer of the Gordons, Major White (later General Sir George White, V.C., the hero of Ladysmith). With a mixed force of Gordons, Seaforths, Gurkhas and Sikhs he feinted towards the gap while the right of the army advanced up the ridge towards the main bulk of the enemy.

By mid-afternoon both wings of Roberts' army had triumphed, and, despite having to bear the brunt of murderous enemy fire from above their positions, they did so at the cost of only eighteen killed and seventy wounded. In the midst of the fiercest fighting the headquarters detachment of the Gordons, then under the command of Lieutenant-Colonel Parker, came under continuous fire from an isolated outpost of tribesmen. A patrol, under the command of Lieutenant Grant and Hector Macdonald, was sent out to dislodge the enemy, an action that caused them no little difficulty as the regimental description of the action makes clear: "They had to climb a bare hill, so steep that they were sometimes on all fours, the enemy firing down on them the while, but when the Highlanders, breathless as they were, reached the top they soon cleared it of the enemy. They were reinforced by a company of the 67th, who brought them meat and drink, and held the hill, being occasionally fired at, till the morning, when they rejoined the column as it marched."[5]

For his part in that action Macdonald was mentioned, with his superior officer, in Roberts' dispatch of 20th October.

> This difficult service was performed in a most gallant manner by a small party of the 92nd, under Lieutenant R. Grant and Colour-Sergeant H. Macdonald, a non-commissioned officer, whose excellent and skillful management of a small detachment when opposed to immensely superior numbers in the Hazardarakht defile, was mentioned in my dispatch of the 16th instant, here again distinguished himself.[6]

The way was now open to Kabul and with the abdication of Yakub Khan, Roberts became the British plenipotentiary in Afghanistan, charged with orders to enforce punishments on the Afghans that would be "swift, stern and impressive, without being indiscriminate or immoderate". Finding the task personally repugnant, Roberts appointed a commission of senior officers and they set to work with a vengeance—literally. A handful of plausible Afghans was charged with Cavagnari's murder and hanged on a makeshift gallows erected outside the ruined British residence; others were tied to cannon muzzles and blown apart, often on the flimsiest of evidence, and, at that, usually given by informants. Even the surrounding villages could not escape the British net, and horror stories (denied indignantly by the government, of course) began to percolate back to the British press about atrocities committed on old people, women and children dispossessed in the cold snow of winter. Having won the war, the British were determined, whatever the cost to Afghan humanity or to British self-respect, to hold the peace.

Mindful that even the severity of those measures would hardly encourage the Afghans to like the British oppressors and that revenge would not be long in coming, Roberts looked for a safe place in which to winter his army. Kabul was an open, undefended city, vulnerable to attack on all sides, but it did possess a large fortified area to the north, a huge walled fortress in the shape of a parallelogram called Sherpur. With its massive walls, it provided his army with a perfect cantonment and it was there that the army dug in for the winter. The number of attacks on British and Indian detachments had increased dramatically during December and although Roberts was worried about sacrificing mobility for safety he was equally scared of the spectre that had begun to haunt him—defeat in the field by an Afghan army.

His decision was only just made in time. On the night of 14th December, following a series of bloody skirmishes around Kabul, a large Afghan force moved into Kabul and laid siege to the British and Indian armies inside Sherpur. The attack came on the 23rd, after a day in which the defenders had been alarmed to hear scaling ladders being dragged into position over the frozen snow outside in preparation for the attack, which when it came was made in a mood of high religious exaltation. Later, Roberts was to estimate that around 100,000 Afghans were in the assault on Sherpur, and, although many were to scoff at his claims, other senior officers supported his computation and said that the figure could well have been greater. At the height of the battle, when all seemed lost, a relieving force of 1,500 British infantry and Gurkhas under Brigadier Charles Gough, appeared on the scene and gradually the huge Afghan army scurried off to the hills, to fight another day.

For the British, the peril over, there was Christmas to look forward to, with extra rations and on New Year's Eve, the Gordons and the Seaforths, always friendly rivals, brought in 1880 with the pipes and by marching round the camp proffering Kabul wine and grog to all-comers. Even the commander-in-chief accepted the invitation. "You have always answered when I called on you," Roberts said, "and now I answer your call as readily."[7]

There was also one other pleasant duty for Roberts to perform. Early in the new year the *Army Gazette* announced the promotion of Colour-Sergeant Hector Macdonald to the commissioned rank of sub-lieutenant in the Gordon Highlanders. The promotion had been made on Roberts' recommendation, and in later life a romantic myth was to grow up that the General had summoned the Sergeant to his tent and had boldly offered him the choice of a commission or a Victoria Cross for the part he had played in the Battle of Charasiah. Equally boldly, the sergeant was supposed to have plumped for the commission instead of the coveted "pennyworth of bronze". It's a good story and one that fits in with the myths that had begun to surround any mention of 'Fighting Mac'—for that was the nickname given to Macdonald in Afghanistan and it was the one by which he was to be affectionately known throughout the British army.

The truth is less fanciful. Roberts was in no position to make an offer of that kind, army regulations forbade it, and as the holder of the V.C. himself—he won it during the Indian Mutiny, rescuing his regimental colours—he would not have wanted to demean either the honour or himself by using it as an official bartering piece. Macdonald was made an officer by Roberts because he had shown qualities of leadership that raised him above his fellow men, qualities that made him a perfect choice for a commission in a regiment like the Gordons, with its proud fighting traditions. (Roberts had a particular regard for the 92nd. He had been a close friend of its colonel in 1865, Christian Monteith Hamilton, the father of Ian Hamilton, a subaltern in the 92nd during the Afghan campaign, a friend of Macdonald's and later, in sadder days, the scapegoat for the Dardanelles campaign during the First World War.)

There was, perhaps, another reason why the story is mere fable. When Roberts offered Macdonald the commission in the Gordons, he knew exactly what he was doing. He was not merely obeying the spirit of the Cardwell reforms, neither was he condemning the former colour-sergeant to a life of ostracism and penury. Although he came from the upper classes he was not a wealthy man and one of the reasons for his being in India was, as we have seen, because it was less expensive to serve there than in a home posting. Like Wolseley and Kitchener, he came from the old Anglo-Irish gentry who were usually poorer than their English counterparts and, lacking large private incomes, were consequently more ambitious. As Corelli Barnett has pointed out in his history of the British army, *Britain and her Army, 1509-1970*, the Anglo-Irish gentry was "the nearest thing Britain ever possessed to the Prussian *Junker* class".[8] Roberts, who had followed his father into the army, was an excellent soldier, ambitious, and loved and respected throughout the army which spoke of him affectionately as 'Bobs'. Perhaps, he saw those qualities in Macdonald and felt that by recommending the commission he was offering Macdonald an odds-on chance to fulfill his ambitions.

When Macdonald's promotion was announced, far from slighting him, the Gordons set out to honour their new officer. The men of 'C' company carried him shoulder-high across the camp to the officers' mess and with the pipes striking up 'Cock of the North' each man marched up to salute their comrade before he was delivered over the divide that separated officers from their men. Inside the mess he was given a friendly welcome and presented with a sword by his fellow officers (it still hangs at Rootfield), and to show their continued loyalty the sergeants presented him with a dirk, the short sword carried by all Highland officers. The mood was one of celebration and Macdonald gave no hint that he felt betrayed by being promoted to a rank that no one in his social position could ever before have hoped to reach.

The Cardwell reforms had made it possible for rankers to become officers by taking away the purchasing of commissions, and although the transition was uncommon, it did happen. Quarter-master sergeants became lieutenants in charge of the regimental commissariat or the regimental police, but they tended to be older, more experienced men who took little or no part in the regiment's training duties and were seldom called on to fight. Macdonald was a young man—he was only twenty-seven—and he took his rightful place amongst the company of twelve subalterns on whose shoulders it fell to keep the Gordons in fighting trim.

Snobbery was not a vice in the Gordons (then as now). Most of the officers had family or geographical links with the regiment and they had made it a point of pride that theirs would be an open, friendly regiment. In public speeches Macdonald was to say that he found himself amongst comrades when he entered the officers' mess and that he never had cause to doubt their sincerity. Certainly his experience was very different from that of the Lincolnshire trooper in the 16th Lancers whose mother had poured such scorn on his going for a soldier—William Robertson. He was promoted to the rank of lieutenant, too, after spending eleven years as a sergeant.

> I'm afraid [he wrote to his father] I do not remember how often I *must* feel cut off from *all* friendship. So far as I know, not *once* has any one in my present sphere taken offence at being in my company, but there is much difference between this and sincere mutual interest; this cannot naturally be between a born gentleman and one who is only now beginning to *try* to become one.[9]

For Robertson, who chose to continue in the cavalry and was destined to rise to the rank of field-marshal, it was a formidable task to become the gentleman that was expected of the officer, but for Macdonald, it was less difficult—although, admittedly, never easy. In a foot regiment like the Gordons it was expected that an officer would be in possession of a private income of around £200 a year. That sum could be augmented for the poorer officers by salary and by additional payments for service overseas. The uniform, with all its variations for service and mess wear was very expensive but, while in Afghanistan, the Gordons' officers wore trews and simple goatskin jackets—it was only when he returned to Britain on depot duty that Macdonald was to feel the financial pinch and, as we shall see, to get into difficulties on that score.

What he had done was to leave the security of the non-commissioned ranks in which all men received their rations of bread and meat, and were clothed from head to foot with all necessary articles from a greatcoat to a toothbrush and those would all be renewed at regular intervals. Now he would have to pay for most of those essentials out of his own pocket as well as indulging himself in some modest entertaining in the mess. Equally importantly, he had cut himself off from his former comrades and, although the Gordons were not themselves stuffy, he would have to mingle with more ethereal beings from other regiments who were uninterested in social or political change.

> After the 1880s the Victorian public schools began to infect the officer corps with their own very narrow snobbery and rigid sense of form . . the control of the army remained in the hands of men out of touch with, and out of sympathy with, the social and technical changes of the age. Secondly, since both officers and men were recruited from unrepresentative social groups, the nation as a whole had little directly to do with the army . . . what cheaper or less troublesome way of running a great empire could there be than a professional army whose officers all had private incomes, and whose rank-and-file were all paupers?[10]

If that was a daunting prospect it should be said that Macdonald himself was an ambitious man, hungry for glory and advancement and he was well aware that the opportunity to shine would be given greater impetus if he was wearing a lieutenant's uniform. It may well have been a social minefield, but on that January day in an alien land, Macdonald must have felt that he had the courage—and the ambition —to cross it.

As Spring came to Afghanistan all appeared to be quiet and to the British it seemed as if their tactics had finally repressed the fiercely patriotic tribesmen. Command of the army had passed to Sir Donald Stewart who established a garrison at Kandahar under Major-General James Primrose and dispatched a force under General Burrowes to Maiwand in southern Afghanistan. Disaster overcame both armies. Burrowes' army was annihilated in July by the Afghans under Ayub Khan, Yakub Khan's younger brother, and when the news reached Kabul it sent a shock of dismay through Stewart's staff. Out of 2,746 men, 934 had been killed and 175 wounded: for British military pride in an occupied country, it was a sorry blow. Then came the news that Primrose and his army was besieged inside Kandahar.

The British public at home was in an uproar about the tragedies and, as so often happens when things go wrong, they demanded a hero and found one in 'Bobs'. He gathered together an army of almost 10,000 men, made up of Gordons, Seaforths, Punjab infantry and cavalry, Gurkhas and Sikhs and a battalion of the 60th Rifles and set out on the immortal march from Kabul to Kandahar. It took them twenty-three days to cover the three hundred and fifty miles and for much of that time Roberts was obliged to keep his movements secret. For the men it was a hard, challenging time, especially for the Gordons who brought up the rear guard and provided the military escort for General Roberts. "An interval of ten paces when in column of fours, was always kept between each company to allow of air, while, if the ground permitted, they marched in open column of companies. A halt was called for ten minutes at the end of each hour, prolonged to twenty minutes at eight o'clock for a snack, the men carrying food in their haversacks, with coffee or tea in their water bottles, and each had occasionally a tot of rum at night. Men who fell out on the march were mounted on ponies but the few who did so were unmercifully 'chaffed' by their comrades, and they got no rum."[11]

On the 31st August 1880 the relief force reached Kandahar to find a garrison so dispirited they lacked the will to fly the Union Jack until Roberts' men came into sight. It only remained for the army to flush out the Afghans from the surrounding hills and at the village of Pir Paimal the Gordons, with White commanding the left flank and Macdonald the right, fought one of the bloodiest actions, a fierce hand-to-hand engagement with a group of tribesmen determined to die to the last man. Those last skirmishes ended the Second Afghan War and having put Abdul Rahman, a nephew of Shere Ali, on the throne, the British withdrew from the country; Roberts was knighted for his services (taking a Gurkha soldier and a Gordon Highlander as the supporters for his coat of arms); and each soldier who took part in the campaign was awarded the Kabul Star and a specially struck medal to commemorate the march from Kabul to Kandahar. And in an act that was, perhaps, worthy of the whole campaign and its senselessness, medals were also presented to Voronel, Roberts' horse, and to Bobbie, the regimental dog of the 66th, Royal Berkshire Regiment.

6

Remember Majuba!

From the wilds of Afghanistan the Gordons marched back to India and arrived at the cantonment at Cawnpore on 5th December when they also received their orders to return home to Britain. Forty-one soldiers decided to stay on in India and were accordingly transferred to other regiments, but for the remaining seven hundred officers and men and their families it was a golden opportunity to look forward to a year or so of garrison duty in Scotland. However, the regiment's calm was shattered on the 6th January 1881 by a telegram from the War Office commanding the Gordons to embark for South Africa where they were needed for Sir Evelyn Wood's army in the Transvaal. "The 92nd Highlanders are to embark for Natal immediately instead of going to England, to be completed in arms and equipment, to take 200 rounds of ammunition per rifle, and the Kabul scale of entrenching tools." Three days later the Gordons arrived at Deolali and on the 14th they embarked on the troopship H.M.S. *Crocodile* bound for Durban.

The decision to send the Gordons to South Africa had been made not so much for strategic reasons but because Sir Evelyn Wood had requested them after receiving a somewhat indiscreet telegram from the subalterns of the regiment. "Personal. From subalterns 92nd Highlanders. Splendid battalion eager service much nearer Natal than England to send. "Although the telegram had been signed by all the subalterns, including Macdonald, the guiding light behind that Biggles-ish ploy was the regiment's senior subaltern, Ian Hamilton. The son of a family with strong connections with the regiment, he had first been commissioned into an English line regiment, the 12th Suffolks, and had transferred to the Gordons when they were lying at Multan in 1874. There he had earned the displeasure of the adjutant by taking an army exam in Hindi to earn the status of an official translator. As his biographer, his nephew, Ian Hamilton, discovered, such a thing was unheard of in the Gordons. "There was a great tradition that the Regiment was everything and any departure from

the sealed pattern was frowned upon. No officer had ever
volunteered for the Staff College, for active service or for anything.
They lived and fought as a regiment, without personal considerations,
which in itself had much to recommend it . . . "[1]

Undaunted by his brother officers' fierce disapproval of breaking
conventions, Hamilton went on to bend several other hoary old rules,
and as a result of his personal bravery, and, from all accounts of his
life, his thoroughly agreeable personality, he soon found friends in
high places. Roberts made him his A.D.C. in 1882, in the Sudan he
was Kitchener's chief-of-staff and he was destined to bring much
honour and distinction to his name. In turn he gave encouragement
and friendship to Macdonald who was a colour-sergeant when first
they met. It had been his duty to teach an exasperated Hamilton the
intricacies of the Gordons' drillbook. To a certain extent those lessons
were wasted—Hamilton remembered that "on parades or field days
we formed ourselves into a square on the smallest provocation, and
(inconceivable idiot that I was) never having properly mastered my
drill, one of my perpetual nightmares was how to extract my
company from the predicament".[2] But Hamilton was to remember
also with gratitude Macdonald's gallantry in battle and his quiet,
gentlemanly bearing.

The regiment's ready acceptance of the order and—although there
is no record of the colonel's views—their tacit agreement that the
subalterns had not acted out of turn was of enormous assistance to
Macdonald. Warfare suited him; it gave him the chance to shine and,
hungry for further honours, he shared his fellow officers' view that
the coming battle with the Boers would be a carefree picnic. On the
Crocodile, as it steamed west across the Indian Ocean, the talk
amongst the Gordons was only of how pleasing it was to be able to
indulge in another scrap before returning home. No one knew much
about the enemy they were about to face nor, indeed, very much
about South Africa and its political problems. The officers of the
Gordons considered it to be a point of pride that they kept an a-
political mess, and a knowledge of current affairs was thought to be
subversive and something to be avoided at all costs. At any rate, their
long sojourn in India and Afghanistan would have made it very
difficult for even the keenest non-conformist to have kept abreast of
events in other parts of the Empire.

Even had they been able to follow the recent history of South
Africa it is doubtful that they would have understood the import of
what had been happening. There was not one British politician who
did. As so often happened in the history of Britain's imperial policies
the outbreak of hostilities in the Transvaal had its origins in a

sequence of political errors compounded by official callousness and indifference. Having acquired the territorial rights to the Cape colonies during the Napoleonic wars the British sought to anglicise them without any regard to the cultural rights of the resident Dutch settlers, many of whose families had been in Africa since the seventeenth century. Like the Israelites, the Boers, as they called themselves, had implicit faith in the indivisibility of their cause, and, disliking the British way of doing things, they set off in 1836 in a mass exodus north, to the rougher lands of the interior. There they set up the Orange Free State, while others hardier still crossed the Drakensberg Mountains into the land of the Zulu and called it Natal, the Boers' promised land.

Unable to prevent themselves from interfering in Boer affairs, and stiffened by an upsurge of morality after the abolition of slavery (to which the Boers would not agree) the British annexed Natal in 1843 and thereby sowed the dragon's teeth. Those Boers who would rather have lived in the wilderness than submit to British dominion climbed into their wagons, trekked across the River Vaal to establish the Transvaal republic and by the Sands River Convention of 1852 were guaranteed their independence by Britain. There the Boers farmed in small communities and established their tight, presbyterian forms of religion (one sect, the Doppers, believed the earth to be flat) and life might have continued in its pastoral, backward way had it not been for the discovery of gold and diamonds in the Transvaal. Under their president, Thomas Burgers, the Transvaal began its own long trek into the nineteenth century but lacking the mechanism of capitalism the country soon found itself bankrupt in 1877—only 12/6d remained in the treasury—and the Transvaal, "for its own protection" was annexed by Britain.

Although that move was welcomed by many, the hardline Boers, men like Paul Kruger and Pieter Joubert, resisted immediately and pleaded with the Colonial Secretary, Sir Michael Hicks Beach, for their country's freedom. However, their resolve foundered in the strength of Prime Minister Disraeli's hope that the white communities would eventually unite in a self-governing confederation on the Canadian model and the Boer leaders returned to the Transvaal where British popularity sank to an all-time low. It plummeted even farther in 1879 when a British force under Lord Chelmsford was routed at Isandhlwana by the Zulus under Cetewayo who had been infuriated by British colonial claims on his kingdom on the Transvaal border.

British pride was restored by the masterful General Sir Garnet Wolseley, one of the few senior British officers who could forsee the future of the new British army and who had supported Cardwell's reforms against the prejudices of the obstinate Duke of Cambridge. Unfortunately for the future of British involvement in South Africa his political prophecies were less successful. Although he had the presence of mind to note to the Colonial Secretary that, "We are hated by nine out of ten Boers with intense hatred", he also told him that "They [the Boers] could not stand up, against our troops for an hour".[3] Within a year the first statement was to be made manifest, and the second a mockery.

When Gladstone's government returned to power in 1880 it was widely expected that it would grant independence to the Transvaal, but a powerful section of the Liberal party had begun to believe that federation was the only solution to the South African problem and thus Gladstone, whose election speeches had included a policy of independence, appeared to the Boers to be reneging on his promises. Unrest, which began as a refusal to pay taxes, gained momentum during the remainder of 1880 and, fired by British indifference to, and derision of, the Boer way of life, open rebellion became a certainty at the year's end when a meeting was held at Paardekraal to proclaim independence for the Transvaal. Kruger was appointed civil leader and Joubert commandant-general. It was an open revolt against the authority of the Crown and it was to be the first successful rebellion since the American War of Independence.

The war began badly for Britain. The weakened army units were defeated by the Boers at Bronkhorstspruit, Ingogo River and Laing's Nek and the public at home were treated to the undignified spectacle of well-trained British soldiers being defeated by what seemed to be an army—if it could be dignified by that name—of ignorant peasant farmers. On one level the public had good reason for concern: the Boers were mobile, expert marksmen and they had the ability to merge deftly with the landscape; but if camouflage and precision shooting were their strongpoints, they were also short of ammunition and badly disciplined, many Boers not thinking twice before drifting off home after a battle. But by their qualities the Boers won a reputation for invincibility in the field and that reputation was to stand them in good stead against the British in the years to come. Of course, the British liked to believe that the Boers won their battles by using unfair and ungentlemanly tactics: at Bronkhorstpruit the Connaught Rangers were cut to pieces in a narrow valley because they refused to withdraw within two minutes of a Boer warning being given.

For Sir George Colley, the commander of the British army it was a nightmare. A brilliant man, almost renaissance in his rounded ability to encompass political economy, military tactics, painting and poetry, he was unaccustomed to the rough and tumble of fighting in the field and during the whole campaign showed a tendency to do things by the book. His military units had been weakened by withdrawal and desertion and it was a bonus to him when Sir Evelyn Wood, who had been sent from Britain to assist him, received the telegram from the subalterns of the Gordons. The regiment arrived in Durban on 30th January and paraded through the town with bayonets drawn and drums beating, a fine sight for the 105 Scottish inhabitants who presented them with an illuminated scroll of welcome. With their pipes and kilts they offered a brave sight to the disheartened British troops who, knowing of the Gordons' exploits in Afghanistan, looked on the Highlanders with awe. Next day they reached Pietermaritz-burg and after receiving another tumultuous welcome, marched up the line to Mount Prospect in the Drakensberg Mountains where Colley had established his headquarters.

The lack of activity, together with the Boers' unwillingness to fight a pitched battle had begun to rankle Colley who was anxious to secure a victory before the inevitable peace settlement—as a senior officer of whom great things were expected, the last thing he wanted was to end the war with a series of humiliating defeats to his name. Colley's problem was that the Boers had entrenched themselves in a narrow defile at Laing's Nek and, having failed once to dislodge them, he could see that the only way to gain tactical advantage was by scaling Majuba Hill, an extinct volcano, 6,500 feet above sea level, which overlooked the Boer camp. To add to his problems, he was also handicapped by the political manoeuvering that had been put in hand by a British government anxious to avoid further bloodshed in South Africa, and, indeed, Colley had been instructed to tell Kruger that if the Boers stopped their opposition, a commission would be established to deal with their case. This was despatched on 21st February with a forty-eight hour time limit.

No answer was received from Kruger—who showed his dis-pleasure at the meagre proposals by trekking north to Rustenburg to deal with a native uprising—and so Colley was caught in a dilemma: if he pressed home an attack he could stand accused of breaking the terms of the British offer. But an officer of Colley's judgement must have known that the Boers would be regrouping, and, so, to defend his own position, he determined to take Majuba on Saturday 26th February. The subsequent battle and its aftermath was to be a subject of much confusion inside and without the army, with many contradictory reports about what did and what did not happen. But, happily, Major White of the Gordons later asked each of the

Gordons' officers who participated in the battle to write down their impressions and from the White Papers a vivid picture emerges of the mixture of stupidity and heroism that was shown that grim weekend. Macdonald, in particular was left in no doubt either about the military qualities or the personal attributes of the men he was fighting. "These men are gentlemen," he said,[4] a point of view which was not held by many of his fellow officers who chose to call the Boers, contemptuously, 'Pinheads'.

Instead of taking the entire regiment of experienced Gordons, Colley decided to choose a mixed force of men from the 56th and 60th regiments, sixty-four men from the Naval Brigade and a detachment of 180 men from the Gordons under the command of Major Hay with three companies under Lieutenants Hamilton, Wright and Macdonald. Although Majuba was to be a disaster for British arms, each of the Gordons officers was to distinguish himself during the course of the battle. Without telling them their final destination, Colley led the 627 men and 22 officers up the steep slopes of Majuba, a march made difficult because it was undertaken in total darkness and because of the heavy loads assigned to the men: each soldier carried rations for six days, water, a blanket, waterproof shelter, greatcoat, seventy rounds of ammunition and each company had to carry a supply of entrenching tools. Stupidly, Colley decided against rocket tubes or Gatling guns. "It was a fearful climb," said Lieutenant Macbean, the Gordons officer who later had the distasteful charge of the burial parties, "and it is a perfect mystery to me how men with pouches full of ammunition, carrying rolled blankets and greatcoat, could ever have got up in daylight, much less on a pitch dark night."[5]

When they eventually reached the summit, the exhausted soldiers discovered a saucer-shaped plateau from which they had a glorious view of the surrounding Drakensberg range and, more importantly, of the Boer camp below. Macdonald was ordered to hold the southern spur of the hill with twenty men and Hamilton a spur to the west, with the remainder of the Gordons, under Hay, on the ridge overlooking the Boer camp. The 58th guarded the eastern edge with the sailors at their left flank. Colley gave no further orders and retired to snatch a few hours' sleep. All would have been well had his men followed suit but at daybreak the Highlanders on the western ridge started to taunt the Boers in the camp below. "Ha ha, got you this time," they shouted, waving their fists. "Come up you beggars, and fight." They were too far away to be heard but their red coats and gleaming buttons were clearly visible to the enemy. Any element of surprise had been lost.

Joubert, the Boer commander, realised that he stood in grave danger while the British held Majuba and he determined to storm it. Three parties under Nicholas Smit and composed mainly of young farmhands were formed at 9.30a.m. and the ascent began. Climbing slowly in a zig-zag pattern and taking cover behind the rocks while their sharpshooters guarded them, the Boers made their way cautiously up the steep slopes. To the British it was an act of folly and only Hamilton on the western ridge showed any inclination to warn Colley of the danger that was facing them. Within the protective saucer of the summit, though, a feeling of carefree confidence had been engendered by the sound of bullets flying harmlessly overhead: men opened their rations, laughed and joked at this, the latest Pinhead madness and turned over to relax in the sunshine. Colley sent a heliograph message to Mount Prospect. "All very comfortable. Boers wasting ammunition. One man wounded in foot."

By eleven o'clock the Boers were within range of the Gordons' line and were beginning to extract a heavy toll on the Highlanders. Unable to return the fire of the hidden enemy, Hamilton asked Colley's permission to fix bayonets and charge, but the answer came back: "Not yet, wait until they cross the open, and then we will give them a volley and a charge." As if the Boers would surrender the advantage of their cover! In his official report to the regiment, Macdonald complained of the frustration of standing by and watching men drop like ninepins along the western ridge. "Lieutenant Macdonald told the writer that he could not have believed, had he not witnessed it, that human nature could have borne what was borne without complaint, beyond the wish expressed to charge down on the invisible enemy . . . he was constantly listening for the sound of guns in an attack on the Nek, to which he supposed the occupation of Majuba was preparatory."[6] Whether or not that was Colley's intention we have no way of telling, for, shortly afterwards, the heliograph messages came to a halt and the remainder of the army in Mount Prospect was left to wonder at their comrades' progress and to bemoan their luck at being left out of the scrap.

Shortly before lunchtime, some of Colley's calm was shattered by the death of Commander Romilly, the officer commanding the Naval Brigade, who was killed in circumstances verging on the farcical. Like Colley he was wearing full staff dress and was a conspicuous target but the manner of his death owed more to ill luck than to bad judgement. While standing on the western ridge he peered over the edge to look at the advancing enemy. "I say," he declared, "there's a man who looks as if he's going to shoot at us. I wonder what the distance is?" His companion Colonel Stewart, raised his binoculars and no sooner had he answered. "Nine hundred yards, I should say", than a Boer bullet hit the unfortunate Romilly in the neck, mortally wounding him.

By 1.30p.m. chaos reigned supreme in the British camp. The Highlanders, unaccustomed to bearing the brunt of hidden fire and furious that a charge was forbidden them, had begun to waver. As the Boers began to reach the summit and to fire round after wilting round into their ranks, the Gordons began to turn tail and run. Confused orders—Hay and his fellow officers said later that Colley had given the command to retire—were shouted amidst the maelstrom of bullets, curses and screams, but the men could not hear them or could not make sense of them. The Highlanders, despite Hamilton's exhortations, broke rank and began the perilous descent of Majuba taking with them the remnants of the 58th and the Naval Brigade. Of the 180 officers and men of the Gordons who climbed Majuba, forty-four died there or as a result of wounds and fifty-two were seriously wounded. It was hardly a rout, and very few men were found dead with bullet wounds in their backs, but it was a bleak day for Highland pride. In the years to come to mention Majuba to a Gordon was to invite a short, sharp reply with the fist.

In the midst of the panic and the confusion there were also men who behaved with courage and dignity. Ian Hamilton rallied his men until shot through the wrist and bleeding heavily he fell to the ground and would have been finished off by a young Boer picket had not an elderly Boer farmer come to his rescue and pushed the youngster aside. (For his work that day Hamilton was recommended for a Victoria Cross, a recommendation that was turned down because he was considered to be too young and his chance would come again. Later in life he was again recommended but turned down, on that occasion because he was too senior.) In his dispatch of 9th March, Sir Evelyn Wood mentioned Private John Murray of the Gordons and put him up for the Distinguished Service Medal.

> Private John Murray was close to the brow over our line of advance during the final forward movement of the Boers. A Scotsman in the Boer ranks called upon Private Murray to surrender. The latter replied, "I'll see you d----d first," and jumped down receiving a bullet wound in the arm. Half-way down the hill his knee fell out of joint, but obtaining the assistance of a comrade to restore it to place, he returned at six o'clock with his rifle and side-arms to camp, where he was seen by Second-Lieutenant Sinclair Wemyss, 92nd Highlanders.[7]

That same dispatch also noted "the conspicuous gallantry displayed by Second-Lieutenant Macdonald "who had held the southern spur of the hill, scorning surrender. His men had come under blistering fire from the Boers before they were able to retaliate. With eight dead and three wounded during that initial onslaught, he ordered the remainder to stand firm and successfully encouraged some of the retreating left flank to follow suit. Remembering Macdonald's success during the skirmish in the Shutargardan Pass, some stayed to fight but they stood little chance, dying one by one in the hail of fire, until only Macdonald and his lance-corporal remained. Down to their last round, he and his companion hurled rocks at the approaching enemy and Macdonald would have continued the fight with the six remaining rounds in his revolver had not the Boers persuaded him to surrender. Out of that incident a new legend was added to Fighting Mac's name.

> Several of the Boers approached Macdonald with the view of taking him prisoner. One, more venturesome than the rest, sprang forward and clutched Macdonald's sporran. Macdonald could not stand this piece of undue familiarity, and consequently gave the Boer a good kick on the stomach, which sent him sprawling on the hill. Just as this Boer was regaining his feet, another levelled his rifle at Macdonald's head, but the would-be robber of the sporran put his friend's rifle away with his hand, saying, "No, no; don't slay him—this man is too good to kill", and then they took Macdonald prisoner.[8]

The incident was remembered and told by the Duke of Atholl in 1899 at a dinner given by the Highland Society of London to honour Macdonald's achievements in the Sudan, and the duke was moved to add that the Boers "found out that Macdonald came from the country in which they play football!"

Later in the day Macdonald was ushered into the presence of General Joubert while arrangements were made for his release. There was an immediate sympathy between the two men. Both were brave, god-fearing soldiers from narrow, Calvinist backgrounds, and, after reading the inscription on Macdonald's sword, there was respect in Joubert's voice as he returned it to him. "A man who has won such a sword should not be separated from it." Macdonald replied with the courteous thought that it was indeed God who had helped the Boers to win the day and they were right to sing psalms after the battle. That point was reinforced by Ian Hamilton who, when he told Joubert, "This is bad day for us", received the reply, "What can you expect from fighting on a Sunday?"[9]

For fighting on a Sunday, poor George Colley was killed, without achieving his ambition of adding a victory to his name. He fell shortly after the Gordons' line broke, a Boer bullet through his head, and his death was not without controversy. There were those—anxious no doubt to save their own tattered reputations—who swore that Colley had given the order to surrender and was reaching for a white handkerchef when he was hit. Others swore that his back was riddled with bullets as he himself tried to flee. If surrender or flight was on his mind—and it is difficult to believe that a man of Colley's calibre would have considered either option—the thought was extingushed as soon as the bullet smashed into his head, removing most of the cranium. Hamilton was asked to identify the body which was removed to the Boer camp at Lang's Nek. There, Colley, still in his staff uniform and wearing the carpet slippers that he had sworn were the best footwear for climbing a hill at night, was guarded by a picquet of Gordons' prisoners under the command of Fighting Mac.

On the Strength

Shortly after the arrangements for their transfer had been completed Macdonald and the other prisoners were returned to their regiments, but not before they had spent some time in Pretoria being questioned by the Boer leaders. Back at Mount Prospect, in the aftermath of the battle, quarrels broke out amongst the soldiers as the men of the 60th Rifles taunted the battered Gordons that things would have been very different had they held Majuba instead of the Scots. But recriminations could not bring Colley back to life, neither would they help the future of the British cause in South Africa. Everyone was sorry that Colley had died an unnecessary death and amongst the politicians at Westminster it was generally agreed that the sooner peace was made, the better it would be for Britain and her imperial policies in the whole of the continent of Africa. Strangely, the defeat at Majuba caused little sensation in London, although in Dublin, nationalist newspapers were quick to point out that a victory for the Boers was also a fillip to the Irish cause.

The negotiations were carried out by Sir Evelyn Wood who managed to talk round the Boers to accepting a British withdrawal from the Transvaal and an inevitable Royal Commission to look into their grievances. Peace might have been established and further bloodshed avoided, but the Liberals' policy for confederation had to be abandoned. More importantly, a feeling grew within the British army that the treaty was without honour, that a military solution was possible and that, sooner or later, Majuba would have to be avenged. In the Second Boer War of 1899-1901, while he was commanding the Highland Brigade, Macdonald turned to a young bugler and said, "You are now on the right road for your father's grave, but I hope, my lad, you'll see it all wiped out."[1] And when the Gordons charged at Elandslaagte, to drive off the Boers at bayonet point, the cry was "Remember Majuba!"

For the Gordons Majuba was their last engagement in South Africa until they returned in 1899 to fight again and to retrieve their lost

without the customary civic receptions or marchpasts. Another factor
which dampened their ardour was the order to remain in Portsmouth
at the Anglesea Barracks until October when they embarked on the
short sea journey to Granton, one of Edinburgh's harbours on the
estuary of the River Forth. From that busy port—it had been
modernised in 1838 and still carried the unique railway ferries across
the Forth to Burntisland in Fife—the Gordons marched up to
Edinburgh Castle with drums and pipes playing and cheering crowds
lined every part of the route. They were destined to stay in
Edinburgh a short twenty months recruiting men from the north-east
where depots had been established in Aberdeen and at Fort George,
and carrying out ceremonial and garrison duties with the 93rd
Highlanders who were also stationed in the castle at the same time.

Meanwhile, the first battalion proceeded to Egypt to take part in
the hostilities that had broken out after Britain had decided to
interfere in that country's affairs. The problem had arisen when
European financiers had lent large sums of money to the Khedive (at
very rewarding interest rates to them); but when they began to
suggest internal economies within the country, there were still
Egyptians to be found who valued their homeland more than
Mammon. A revolt by Colonel Ahmed Arabi—a Nasser before his
time who believed that Egypt should be for the Egyptians—
threatened British stability in the area and made a puppet of the
Khedive. Seeing the danger to their funds, and more importantly, to
the Suez Canal, the British launched a punitive expedition under Sir
Garnet Wolseley and so began sixteen years of involvement there
and in the Sudan. Several officers in Edinburgh transferred to the
first battalion to see some of the action while one or two others took
advantage of the opportunity of being transferred to the Egyptian
army after its subjugation at the Battle of Tel-el-Kebir early in 1883.

Although that was to be a theatre of war which Macdonald was to
know intimately in the coming years, he remained with the second
battalion in Edinburgh. He had been promoted full lieutenant on 1st
July 1881 and while in Scotland he took on the additional
responsibilities of quartermaster, in which capacity he was seconded
for a short period to the Commissariat Staff in Belfast. Those
additional duties hardly added to his status but at least they brought
him much-needed funds, for it was during that period of home leave
that Macdonald began to run into financial difficulties. Having spent
most of his soldiering life under canvas and, as an officer in the field,
with the bare essentials of uniform, he suddenly found himself
having to cope with the purchase of expensive items of uniform.
While the corporals and colour sergeants swaggered in their kilts

down to the taverns and brothels that stood in the closes and wynds off the neighbouring Royal Mile, Macdonald, cut off from their ranks, had to keep silent counsel in the officers' mess and make what savings he could.

That he managed may be seen in a photograph taken in Edinburgh, probably during the winter of 1883-1884. He stands there, four-square to the world in the red dress jacket, kilt with the officers' sporran adopted by the Gordons after amalgamation, the broach presented to him by the men of 'C' company, white sword belt and court shoes. He looks every inch the officer, but at what cost to himself and to his pride? Although, as we have seen, the Gordons were not a snobbish regiment, several officers were bonnet lairds from the north-east with social connections with the landed gentry of the Lothians and Fife and they could look forward to balls and weekend shooting parties. It had been one thing for Macdonald to carry off an officer's requirements for courage and loyalty in battle; it was quite another for him to measure up to the social *desiderata* of peacetime soldiering. In later life Macdonald was to be made much of by the Scottish upper classes, but in 1883, in the lowly rank of lieutenant, and a poor, unconnected one at that, his social life in Edinburgh perforce had to be cautious and solitary. That money was a problem we know from a letter to his brother William, written shortly before embarking for Egypt, and requesting £30 so that he might not embarrass the regiment's agents.[3] Not for him the swagger of expensively cut clothes and a personal tailor, and throughout his life his civilian appearance was to be a matter of comment to those who knew him only in the heroic pose of an army uniform. T.P. O'Connor knew Fighting Mac well enough, and he liked him too, but this puzzled description, written after Macdonald's death, would have been equally applicable in any year during his commissioned service.

> He was one of those men who ought never to have appeared out of uniform. He gave you the idea of strength and splendid manliness and bulldog power, but there was nothing of distinction in his air, in his manner, or in his dress. He just looked a Tommy, and a Tommy in his Sunday clothes, which is not Tommy at his best. If I remember rightly the clothes were dark, not very well cut, gave you an impression of squareness rather than curves; in short, suggested the bourgeois citizen in his Sunday garb. And the manner was pretty much the same: it lacked distinction.[4]

Later in the article O'Connor went on to praise Macdonald's "quiet simplicity" and "brightness of humour" and in general the writing is sympathetic, even if it cannot quite hide the author's condescension towards an officer whose military strengths belied his civilian weaknesses in the Army and Navy Club in Pall Mall.

Left to his own devices, Macdonald would wander down from the castle to gaze in the shop windows of Princes Street and to take solitary walks along the Water of Leith a small meandering river which runs through the city. Early in 1883, while on one of his walks, he met Christina MacLouchan Duncan, the daughter of a schoolmaster who was at that time living in Frederick Street. Her family came originally from Perthshire and when she met the thirty-year-old subaltern she was completing her education in the city. She was only fifteen. They must have made a strange sight together: the quiet schoolgirl and her solemn chaperone in awkward civilian clothes who met her each day to carry her books home from school. On the 10th July he gave her a birthday present and a worried father quizzed Macdonald about his intentions. When marriage was mentioned, the Duncans hesitated; their daughter was too young; the match would be a poor one; and so it was proposed that an informal engagement be entered into until Christina was older and Macdonald a more senior officer—he would have known, too, that the Gordons had a rule which discouraged marriage before the rank of captain had been reached. However, by the Spring of 1884 events were precipitated by the news that the Gordons were to leave Edinburgh and the couple decided to bring matters forward by going through an irregular form of marriage in the Duncan's house at 2 Kew Terrace in Murrayfield. They married in the old Scots style by pledging their troth to each other with only heaven as their witness. This form of marriage, by declaration *de praesenti,* had become popular in the years after the Reformation in Scotland when marriage became less of a religious bond and more of a legal contract and it was to remain a law of the land until 1939. However, as marriages of that kind usually took place without witnesses, or in front of witnesses who were not impartial, they usually had to be declared legal by ruling of the Court of Session (the central civil court of law in Scotland) and that was the action forced on Christina in 1894.

On the 17th July she appeared before Lord Stormonth-Darling to solemnise the marriage that had remained a secret for so long, and in *The Scotsman* the following day a report appeared in which Christina said that in 1883 and 1884 Macdonald "had visited constantly at her father's house, paid her marked attention and made professions of love to her. As a result of these protestations she consented to a marriage taking place between them by exchanging consents. She and he were alone in the room. She understood what she was doing, and understood it was the law if the two persons consented. He took out a Bible and asked her to swear. She said, 'I solemnly swear and declare that I take you, Hector Archibald Macdonald, to be my husband, to love, honour and obey. So help me God.' He in similar terms took her for his wife. They both kissed the Bible. He made her promise that she would not reveal the marriage. There was a child of the marriage. It was six years old. He had sent money to support her and the child, and had behaved very nicely."

Macdonald did not contest the action and the declarator of marriage was granted to his common law wife. Surprisingly, the matter remained a secret, even in 1894 by which time Macdonald was a reasonably well-known name, and the War Office was never informed of the relationship, his next of kin continuing to be listed as his brother William. Between 1884 and 1898 Macdonald was to spend most of his life abroad. He was never to enjoy the benefits of a domestic life and to the world he remained a bachelor and a stern, somewhat forbidding and distant figure. While he was on a short leave in 1886 Christina conceived a child by him and she left Edinburgh to live in England—she could hardly have lived a respectable bourgeois life in Edinburgh with a secret marriage and an all too obvious pregnancy. In a letter to Dingwall Town Council after her husband's death she explained that they had "arranged that until Hector's education was completed we should live very quietly and when the sad event occurred I was living at Dulwich where Hector was at college".[5] Their son, Hector Duncan Macdonald had been born in 1887 and to all intents and purposes his birth was the sum of their sexual relationship. The secrecy of their 'marriage' in Edinburgh with domestic circumstances preventing any intimacy, and the couple's consequent separation, would have seen to that: in the years to come he would only see her briefly while on leave in 1886, again; briefly in 1892, when he also visited Rootfield, on his triumphant return after Omdurman in 1899, and finally in 1903 before leaving for his last journey back to Ceylon.

As a professional soldier and a recently gazetted lieutenant, Macdonald had good reason to keep quiet about his marriage. The Gordons, discouraged marriage and other regiments, too, looked on it as being detrimental to a soldier's career. The Cameronians, for example, had a mess rule that an officer would be fined £50 if he married before being promoted captain and pointed out with some pride that their second battalion possessed only two married officers. It was generally agreed that a married soldier was a less than efficient member of a regiment and that to do his duty to the best of his ability the good officer had to be free of domestic responsibilities. Besides, being a soldier in Victorian times was a dangerous business and it was thought to be unfair to expose married men to the constant dangers of warfare or tropical disease in the service of Empire. (Another school thought it likely that married men would hold themselves back in battle for fear of destituting their widows.) And so the officers' mess of many regiments became the retreat of elderly bachelors who preached the monogamous life to new recruits in much the same way that a Catholic priest would uphold celibacy as a virtue. Of course, for the army officer the torments of fleshly lust were easily assuaged with a visit to a brothel for unemotional sex.

For the Victorian man, sex was a paradox. On the one hand he was supposed to keep himself pure for the delights of wedded bliss and, to offer moral support, countless tracts thundered against the damaging delights of masturbation, wet dreams and going with prostitutes of either sex. Epilepsy, impotence, consumption, blindness, paralysis and eventual madness were only some of the results of practising those secret vices and sex was a hidden, dangerous urge, capable of ruining any man who lost control of his desires. Yet, although some doctors portrayed the man who indulged in "beastliness" as "the pale complexion, the emaciated form, the slouching gait, the clammy palm, the glassy or leaden eye, and the averted gaze indicate the lunatic victim to this vice"[6], others also counselled that abstention from sex could lead to impotence or worse, and so prostitution flourished. With sex outside marriage virtually impossible within one's own class, many middle class men turned to commercial sex as the alternative to total abstinence. (And prostitutes in turn caused a fresh problem for their clients: men discovered in the girls' sexual abandon the fear that they might be confronted by a sexually demanding woman in marriage.) It was a sordid enough business by any standards.

> There need, however, be no hesitation in saying that Saturday night in the High Street and Canongate of Edinburgh presents one of the most revolting sights ever witnessed. The filth, degradation and utter hopeless misery presented to view is awful, and in no city is it possible that it could be exceeded; indeed it may be gravely questioned if in any city, in one night of the week, destitution, prostitution and crime ever held such a review as they hold in the High Street of the Modern Athens.[7]

Edinburgh, though, was by no means alone in having an underworld of prostitution and the crime that went with it. London had its share of criminals and prostitutes who haunted Drury Lane and Covent Garden and who were as much part of the passing scene for the *haut monde* of Mayfair and the inhabitants of the new

Pooterish suburbs south of the River Thames as were the new-fangled horse omnibuses. In fact, hardly a major city in Britain was without its fair share of prostitutes and it was to them that the Victorian male would turn for comfort. Brothels flourished near barracks and in harbour areas where soldiers and sailors provided easy earnings for the prostitute and her madame or 'flash' man. Even abroad, the regiments of the British army encouraged official brothels in which the threat of venereal disease and racketeering could be kept to a minimum, as Frank Richards was candid enough to remember in his memoirs of army life in India.

> For the benefit of our health, because it was said that to abstain was unhealthy in a hot climate, the Prayer-wallah and I occasionally visited the Rag [official brothel]. I took every precaution, for which I am truly thankful, and most of the other signallers did the same; but no man that ever breathed ever took more precautions than what the Prayer-wallah did. In addition to antiseptics and prophylactics he possessed a powerful magnifying glass which he used to handle with the professional manner of an old family doctor. He could never understand why the Indian government did not issue every man in India with one the same. He said that it was of far more benefit to him than his tooth brush, about which so much was spoken in the addresses on Personal Cleanliness that we were sometimes given. Whenever he appeared in the Rag Street the girls he had been with before would shout: "Hello, my Spy-glass wallah!"[8]

Sex may have been a taboo subject for the Victorian man but its urges were obviously given careful consideration by the forward planners of the new army. From that background of male hypocrisy a new version of female sexuality was born: the woman as angel-mother or as sweet, adorable child. In both cases the woman was seen as a frail creature, capable only of pure, untainted love, to be put on pedestals and worshipped from afar. Writers like Tennyson, Thackeray and Browning—even Thomas Carlyle admitted that "it was the earliest terror of my childhood that I might loose my mother"—sanctified the ideal of motherhood as the most glorious of human loves and the woman as mother reached its zenith, perhaps, in the figure of Queen Victoria, the 'Mother of the Empire'. Robert Louis Stevenson and J.M. Barrie, both very different writers, fell easily in love with older women and there are other examples of Victorian men who failed to form lasting relationships with women from their age group and preferred to be like one of Barrie's heroes who said, "Just as I was about to fall in love I suddenly found that I preferred the mother."[9]

Allied to this emotional instability was a growing fervour in the final twenty years of the nineteenth century for adorable little girls who offered a trust and innocence far removed from strident female sexuality. Tasteful postcards began to appear of cherubic pink-cheeked girls whose rosebud bodies betrayed no burgeoning signs of maturity, and it became quite common for older men to accompany young girls on visits to the theatre and in other public places. Most famous of these was the Oxford scholar, the Rev. C.L. Dodgson who wrote under the name of Lewis Carroll. He saw nothing immoral in his relationships with young girls—many of whom he photographed, innocently enough, in the nude—and even went so far as to enquire if he was on kissing terms with them:

> Dear Mrs Rowell,   Ch.Ch. Oxford, June 25/95
>
> The being entrusted with the care of Ethel for a day is such a great advance on mere acquaintanceship, that I venture to ask if I may regard myself as on 'kissing' terms with her, as I am with many a girl-friend a great deal older than *she* is. Considering that—she being 17 and I 63—I am quite old enough to be her *grandfather*, I hope you won't think it a very out-of-the-way suggestion. Nevertheless, if I find you think it wiser that we should only shake hands, I shall not be *in the least* hurt. Of course, I shall, unless I hear to the contrary, continue to shake hands only.
>
>   Very truly yours,
>   C.L. Dodgson[10]

Lewis Carroll no doubt suffered from retarded emotional development and failed to understand the urges that led him to idolise the pre-pubic girl (he tended to drop them as 'girl-friends' when they reached maturity) but he had also suffered an unhappy love affair and had turned in later life to the understanding affection that could be granted willingly by little girls.

When Macdonald met Christina in the winter of 1883, the vogue of sentimental love for little girls was reaching its heights in England and even in douce Edinburgh it may have been respectable enough for a grown man to have paid chivalrous court to a young girl. Indeed, it was considered perfectly healthy to have an interest in young people in general. Later, when the accusations of homosexual behaviour were made in Ceylon, people in Edinburgh remembered that the thirty-year-old Macdonald had led groups of admiring young boys up the castle esplanade to teach them the rudiments of drilling and throughout his life he was to enjoy the company of young people. The Boys' Brigade had been founded in 1883 and Macdonald was to follow its progress with interest, frequently taking the time to give speeches and to inspect ceremonial parades. It was something to be proud of—in Edinburgh twenty years earlier the philanthropist John Hope had established a boys' club for marching and drilling known as the 'Water Rats'. Looked after by a group of old soldiers they were a common sight in Scotland's capital and in 1863 they even took part in militia exercises in Holyrood Park where they became known as the 'wee warriors'.

Macdonald's homosexuality will be discussed in a later chapter but it seems unlikely that his interest in young people would have made him an invert. His contemporary, and fellow officer in South Africa, Robert Baden-Powell, founded the Boy Scouts in 1907 to universal approval and during the Victorian and Edwardian periods when service to Empire was a paramount public virtue, manly encouragement given to young boys was considered to be good form for a man in Macdonald's position. In short, he was only obeying the spirit of the age. Probably emotionally backward—although there is evidence in one biographical sketch of an early love affair in Dingwall with a girl called Bella Mackay—his lack of sexual experience and his awkwardness with women of the middle classes led him to turn to the angel figure of a young girl for his wife.

Christina married when she was only sixteen and in an age when it was the custom for middle-class women (and frequently men too) to be painfully misinformed about sexual matters: we can be fairly certain that she was naive in that respect. In most respectable homes sex was not a subject for polite discussion, ignorance of bodily function led to a morbid fear of sex and most women went to their marriage beds unaware of the physical relationship into which they were entering. It became for them a 'necessary ordeal': "I incline to the belief that any right-thinking man would prefer to feel that his bride knew the sacrifice she must make of her person to his natural demands, and that her confidence in him was sufficient to enable her to face the necessary ordeal."[11] And if that came from one of the better guides to marriage and is off-putting enough, then it must be remembered that most marriage manuals ignored the subject completely. Thus, in many middle-class Victorian marriages sex became a frightening experience and if the woman gained any pleasure at all there were always prudes at hand ready to whisper that only the lascivious or fallen woman actually enjoyed sex with her husband.

Allied to the general air of loathing and ignorance was a more or less complete lack of knowledge of contraceptive methods and so sex also brought with it the added fear of pregnancy. Childbirth was usually a painful business, with clumsy medical techniques child mortality rates were unnecessarily high, and a large family could be a strain on domestic finances. For most middle-class Victorian women—and from what is known about her background Christina Duncan was a typical example—marriage and the sexual relationship it brought with it could be a frightening ordeal. Many women could not face sex again after the experience of the first night of marriage and many marriages were never consummated at all, due to the ignorance of both parties. A husband was 'good' or 'understanding' if he refrained from insisting on a vigorous sex life with his wife, and chastity within marriage became an accepted fact of life for many couples. Although neither Macdonald nor his wife left any record of their feelings on the subject, given the furtiveness of their marriage, the long years of separation and the lack of opportunity—they only saw one another on four brief occasions during nineteen years of marriage—it is reasonable to conclude that neither Hector nor Christina gained much sexual fulfillment from their relationship.

8

What an accursed country!

At the end of June 1884, the second battalion left Edinburgh by rail for Greenock where it joined the troopship H.M.S. *Assistance* bound for Devonport. During the stay at Raglan Barracks before leaving for garrison duty in Guernsey, the Gordons were paid an official visit by General Roberts before he himself left Britain to take up his new appointment as commander-in-chief of the army in India, and it was typical of the man who had commissioned Macdonald that he should have taken the opportunity of being present at a similar ceremony when Corporal Beresford of the Gordons was promoted lieutenant and transferred to the Royal Irish Rifles.

When the battalion moved to Guernsey on the 11th December 1885, Macdonald was not of their number. Eighteen months earlier he had transferred to the first battalion with Major White and three other officers to see active service in Egypt where the Gordons had been selected to be part of Lord Wolseley's 7,000 strong force to relieve General Gordon in Khartoum in the Sudan. The story of that mournful episode is one of the most pathetic in British imperial history and in one sense it typifies all that was wrong in the country's attitudes not only to her colonies but also to other countries which Britain thought should be brought under the *Pax Britannica*. By stifling the Egyptian uprising at Tel-el-Kebir Britain might have subdued national pride and made a puppet of the Khedive but she had also inherited Egypt's long-standing problem: the neighbouring Sudan; and just as the government in India had found it impossible to interfere successfully in Afghanistan, so too did the Egyptian administration quail before the Sudan and the difficulties thrown up by its terrain and inhospitable desert tribes.

Although Gladstone's Liberal administration had set its face against intervention in the Sudan, it could not control many of its policies at a local level and it was that failure that was to contribute to a fifteen-year series of little wars and bloody campaigns on the banks of the River Nile. It had become the custom for Britain to loan officers from her own army to the armies of subject nations or to countries friendly to her and several British officers, fired by ambition and the higher ranks and rates of pay, had transferred to an Egyptian army that was still disillusioned and demoralised after its thrashing at Tel-el-Kebir. Initially, the standard of those officers was very low, many were rejects who could not find a suitable niche in British regiments and their command of Egyptian troops in the Sudan between 1883 and 1884 led to a number of pathetic defeats by the desert tribesmen who had united behind the Mahdi. This magnetic man, El Mahdi, or the messiah to his followers, had rallied together a mighty army of Dervishes—fierce tribesmen willing to fight to the death to preserve their faith—to rid the Sudan of the hated Egyptians. Ranged alongside them was the forceful ruler of the eastern Sudan, Osman Digna, an able military leader who inflicted two crushing defeats on the cowardly Egyptian forces at El Teb and Sinkat in the early part of 1884. He was a man who managed to put the fear of death, into his enemies.

Although those skirmishes meant little to the furtherance of British imperial policy, pride was involved and it became necessary in military eyes, to teach the 'fuzzy-wuzzies' (as the Dervishes were known by the British troops) a lesson. Accordingly, after the lesson had been administered at the battle of Tamai, the British sent a governor-general to Khartoum to arrange the orderly evacuation of British and Egyptian citizens from the Sudan. His name was General Charles Gordon, later to be immortalised as a martyr of empire and an upholder of Christian virtue in the face of the savage heathen. A Christian mystic, Gordon was considered to have been one of Britain's best leaders of irregular native troops and his exploits in China, fighting Taiping rebels on behalf of the Shanghai merchants had earned him the title of honorary mandarin and throughout the army he was known as 'Chinese' Gordon. He seemed to bear a charmed life; his fearless heroism had made him a public favourite and his appointment to the Sudan was hailed with much satisfaction. But Gordon was also something of an eccentric. Sir Evelyn Baring, later to become Lord Cromer, thought him "half cracked", and Lord Northbrook spoke of him as a "mad man"; and his personal behaviour was a matter of no little speculation. Little boys were the object of his special delight and although he might have shrunk from sexual relationships with them, his religious fervour led him to open his English residence to tend for poor boys and orphans. His energy may have come from the asceticism of his religious beliefs but he took a good deal of pleasure from bathing his charges himself and then drying them in front of mirrors that they might view their inner and outer cleanliness. "That he was a practising sodomite is extremely improbable", opined his latest biographer, Charles Chenevix Trench[1], but his interests in young people, coupled with an almost manic religious fanaticism and a morbid hypochondria, make Gordon a somewhat unusual Victorian hero and help, perhaps, to put into perspective Macdonald's own sexual inclinations.

Having taken up residence at Khartoum, Gordon began to feel the manifest destiny of his mission, which he believed lay in the integrity of his Christianity and officer class *mores* against the heathen devilry of the Mahdists. When the Dervish army besieged Khartoum, Gordon could have escaped but he saw that it was his divine duty to stay while politicians at home argued about what was to be done in the Sudan. After a good deal of prognostication Gladstone, urged on by a public clamorous for Gordon's safety, ordered Wolseley to repair with all speed to the relief of Khartoum and it was to that force, in the uniform of an officer of the first battalion of the Gordons that Macdonald was assigned in September 1884. With his experience of administration in Edinburgh and Belfast behind him, he was appointed adjutant at the fort of Assiout, the town from which the boats carrying the river column set out up the river Nile towards Khartoum. Another force—the desert column—went overland but through a sequence of bad preparations, difficulties with the unwieldy boats and niggling skirmishes with enemy forces, Wolseley's army arrived too late and Gordon and his compatriots were slaughtered in Khartoum on 26th January 1885. That incident brought to an end British interest in the Sudan for the time being, but like Majuba it was to be source of much rancour for the officers who had taken part in the expedition and revenge for Gordon's murder was to be uppermost in many military minds in the years to come.

The death of the Mahdi in the summer of 1885 and increased agitation on the Afghanistan border with India helped to dampen public enthusiasm for a war of revenge in the Sudan and in the lull that followed, the British authorities in Egypt set about re-equipping and retraining the Egyptian army. The Sirdar, Sir Evelyn Wood, appointed twenty-six British officers to his command and set about re-organising the Egyptian army along British lines, with British officers and a number of non-commissioned officers in key positions. Those men were attracted by three contrasting, but important considerations which had been built into their appointments: promotion to the rank above that held in the British army, a generous rate of pay, and little or nothing to spend in the way of expenses. Amongst their number was Lieutenant Hector Macdonald who, in the local rank of captain, was seconded to the Egyptian Gendarmerie, an extra-ordinary para-military force commanded by Valentine Baker, a remarkable British soldier and friend of the Prince of Wales, whose military career had been wrecked in August 1875 when he was convicted of indecently assaulting a young girl in a railway carriage. The trial caused a sensation, Baker was fined and imprisoned and in the hysteria that followed, railway companies noted a sharp, temporary decline in travellers—women for fear that they might be attacked in similar manner, and men scared of being unwittingly accused. Thus the coming of the railway age brought with it its own contribution to Victorian sexual fantasies.

Baker's life had been devoted to the army. He had started his soldiering in Ceylon, had fought in the Crimean War and, as a keen student of tactics, had been a spectator of the Franco-Prussian war of 1871. At the time of his disgrace he was assistant quartermaster-general at Aldershot and nearing the zenith of his career. But he was too good a soldier to be lost to the army, any army, and after his release and subsequent banishment from English society, Baker became a mercenary in the Turkish army before finding his way down to Egypt to take over command of the Gendarmerie—he would have been given the army but Wood thought that British officers might have resisted serving under a man who had disgraced himself in such a public way. Macdonald, presumably, had no such compunction in serving under Baker and between them they moulded their *fellahin* troops into an adequate fighting force. Drill and discipline were Macdonald's chosen instruments and by the time he transferred to the Egyptian army in January 1888 with the substantive rank of captain in the Gordons, he had discovered the means of instilling loyalty and courage into troops who had shown so little capacity for fighting in the field of battle.

While he was stationed in Cairo, Macdonald first came into contact with a man who many think had an ill-starred influence over his future affairs—Horatio Herbert Kitchener, an aloof young officer of the Royal Engineers who was gaining rapid attention in official circles for his ambitious drive and energy. Born in Ireland in 1850, Kitchener had been educated at home and in Switzerland by his soldier father, and a number of tutors, under barbaric conditions of self-imposed discipline and arbitrary punishment. As a result he had grown into a man possessed of a great deal of high moral purpose and of a belief that "he was defrauding the Almighty if he did not carry out his task".[2] At the time of the Gordon relief expedition, Kitchener had muscled his way into Egypt where his ill-concealed ambition had made him extremely unpopular with Cairo society. His natural shyness and awkwardness with people kept him apart from the *grande dames* who ruled the tight social circles of the European community and his inability to mix was seen by many as yet another example of his arrogant behaviour. Kitchener, though, kept himself to himself and attracted to his company a small circle of friends and admirers who were fiercely loyal to the young brevet-lieutenant-colonel and amongst their number was Valentine Baker whom Kitchener had first met in Turkey.

For the first, and apparently the only time in Kitchener's life he fell in love—with Baker's youngest daughter, Hermione. All his resolutions to remain a bachelor melted away as he basked in the love of this beautiful girl and it was generally expected that an engagement would soon follow. Hermione's death in 1885 put paid to that fond hope but for several years thereafter he continued to wear a gold locket containing her portrait. Much has been written about Kitchener's sexual preferences[3] which were probably those of a natural celibate, as his most able biographer, Sir Philip Magnus, suggests. His attachment to his military secretary Oswald Fitzgerald was the subject of comment, as was his interest in collecting porcelain and his liking for flower arranging, but more importantly, Kitchener believed that he travelled fastest who travelled alone. When he became Sirdar in 1892 he demanded that his British officers be single men, devoted solely to the task in hand.

> Kitchener used personally to interview, with the greatest care, candidates for service in his army, at the Junior United Service Club during his annual visit to England on leave. Those who were successful started with a two years' contract in the rank of major, but Kitchener made marriage, or even an engagement to marry, an absolute bar. He told candidates that marriage interfered with work because it involved a divided loyalty; and he told Cromer there was no reason to pay marriage allowances while suitable single officers were available. He succeeded presently in surrounding himself with an impressive band of extraordinarily youthful colonels who were completely imbued with their chief's methods and ideals.[4]

Thus, Macdonald, who became one of those "youthful colonels", would have known two sides to Kitchener's personality—the fierce martinet who demanded celibacy, and the lovelorn suitor of Baker's daughter. Kitchener's detractors continued to imply that he was a homosexual, unworthy of high rank and that aspect of his character and his relationship to Macdonald was to excite much comment in later and unhappier years. Certainly the influential correspondent Dr George Ernest Morrison was in no two minds about Kitchener and that "band of boys" who accompanied him into the Egyptian army.

He abhorred Kitchener's personal greed and quoted a Reuters'
correspondent who said of Kitchener that, "he drinks and has the
other failing acquired by most Egyptian officers, a taste for buggery".[5]
Drink was not one of Kitchener's failings and the accusation of
pederasty, although interesting in view of Macdonald's case, was
probably caused by the dislike for him that many felt when they first
encountered this trim, elegant man. In fact Kitchener was capable of
exciting a wide range of conflicting emotions. On the one hand were
his close circle of friends and admirers, the "band of boys" who
included the mercurial French-Canadian Edouard Girouard and the
handsome Frank 'Brat' Maxwell V.C.; and there were those like
Winston Churchill who hated Kitchener with a fanaticism equal to
that engendered by those who loved him. "My father was War
Minister before he was thirty seven," said Churchill during a private
after-dinner discussion with Dr Morrison. "Before I am thirty seven I
will be War Minister. There is time for me to get my knife into
Kitchener."[6]

Macdonald's transfer to the Egyptian army in 1888 coincided with
Kitchener's appointment as adjutant-general in Egypt and from then
until Omdurman ten years later the fates of both men were to be
bound inextricably together. One of Kitchener's first tasks while
based in the port of Suakin in the eastern Sudan was to raise three
battalions of Sudanese troops for employment in the army of Egypt.
It was a sound choice because those men, who came principally from
the warlike Shilluk and Dinka tribes on the upper Nile, made superb
soldiers. "Be it observed that the term black in this connection, is *not*,
as is so often, an exaggeration, or a figure of speech," warned Sir
Alfred Milner, later to be Lord Milner, Britain's high commissioner in
South Africa after the Boer War, but then acting as Under-Secretary
for Finance in Egypt, "Not even the most sensitive Radical could
object to the 9th-13th Soudanese being described as 'black men', and
they themselves are rather proud than otherwise of their own hue of
deepest ebony."[7] (Other contemporary authorities cite the Sudanese'
preference for being called 'Blue Men'.)

To Macdonald fell the duty of commanding the 11th Sudanese
battalion and they met their baptism of fire in the debatable lands of
the Sudanese border, pitted in action against the army of Osman
Digna, first at Gemaizeh in December 1888 and again in the following
year at Toski, a battle that thwarted Sudanese ambitions in Egypt. For
his part in the campaign Macdonald was mentioned in dispatches
and awarded the Khedive's Star, a handsome medal that he was to
wear with pride—although he had to wait for Queen Victoria's
permission before adding it to the growing collection on his dress

uniform. As the British had already done in India with the formation of Indian native regiments commanded by British officers, so also did Kitchener's 'boys' weld the Sudanese into a disciplined military machine and they did so by not only appealing to the Sudanese' natural inclination to enjoy fighting but also by trading on the blue men's dislike of the Dervishes. During the Battle of Gemaizeh, Macdonald's battalion had to be restrained from breaking rank and hurling themselves at the enemy, and as G.W. Steevens, the war correspondent of the *Daily Mail*, recorded, it was almost a matter of luck rather than judgement that Macdonald was able to channel his troops' enthusiasm into proper fighting order.

> At Gemaizeh, the 11th, ever anxious to be at the enemy, broke its formation and it is said that Macdonald Bey, after exhausting Arabic and Hindustani, turned in despair to abusing them in broad Scots. Finally he rode up and down in front of their rifles and at last got them steady under a heavy fire from men who would far rather have killed themselves than him.[8]

By treating his men fairly and squarely and by instilling in them the need for discipline Macdonald turned his Sudanese battalion into a fierce fighting unit. At the heart of his training lay his implicit belief in the importance of drilling and his white sergeants attached to the battalion soon found recruits to their ranks who were enthusiastic to the cause of precision drilling. Macdonald himself would help out on those occasions and it became a source of tolerant amusement to the officers commanding the other battalions to see an exasperated Fighting Mac dismount from his charger and take over the parade when sequences and drill movements started to go awry. When he took over the command of the 2nd Sudanese Brigade before Omdurman, Macdonald encouraged them to adopt the traditions of the Scottish regiments and one of his battalions, the 9th, wore the kilts of the Seaforth Highlanders and carried their colours into battle, after fighting side by side with the Scots at the Battle of Ginnis. By then Macdonald was a well-known character in Egypt, capable of drawing out superlatives from even the most hardened and cynical war correspondents.

> In person, 'old Mac'—he is under fifty but anything above forty is old in the Egyptian army—is of middle height, but very broad—so sturdily built that you might imagine him to be armour plated under his clothes. He walks and rides with a resolute solidity bespeaking more strength than agility. He has been known to have fever but never to be unfit for duty.[9]

Remarks of that kind in the British press were to become more familiar to Macdonald as the Sudanese campaign progressed.

Further disturbances along the frontier threatened the uneasy peace but at the back of the minds of all the officers in the Egyptian army was the eventual invasion of the Sudan and the harvesting of sorely-needed revenge for Gordon's murder at Khartoum. Much of the problem facing the high command was a more or less total lack of knowledge of the Sudan, its people and its terrain; and Kitchener, who had himself once worked in intelligence, established an intelligence section under Colonel Reginald Wingate. To begin with Wingate and his officers found it difficult to establish any kind of spy network, so loyal were the Dervishes to their new leader, Khalifa Abdullah, son of the Mahdi, but the breakthrough came in 1891 when a missionary, Father Ohrwalder, made his escape from captivity in Omdurman. He brought with him much-needed information about the Khalifa's rule and its subtleties and cruelties, facts that only served to add to Britain's outraged sense of indignation about the Sudan. It was tacitly assumed that the retraining of the Egyptian army had one end in view: the reconquest of the Sudan—although there were those, like Bennet Burleigh, the *Daily Telegraph's* war correspondent, who doubted if it would be worth the trouble. "What do the British want in this country? Is it the intention of the government to do away with capital punishment and send all felons here? I am not surprised the camel has the hump. I would develop one here myself. What an accursed country!"[10]

Certainly, the conditions of service were trying for officers and men alike. During their years of appointment in Kitchener's army, home leave was banned as an unnecessary luxury, which meant that apart from a short leave in 1892, between 1887 and 1899, the years of his son's, Hector's, childhood, Macdonald was not to leave the deserts of Egypt and the Sudan; and although the pay was good, dysentery and malaria were endemic and death a familiar companion. For the men it was worse. The Egyptian and Sudanese troops were clothed in wretched uniforms made out of inferior materials and their boots— soldiers had to march long distances in those days—were of the poorest quality, all because Kitchener believed that battles should not be a burden on the Egyptian exchequer. It was a policy that was to win applause from the British public but it was not one calculated to wring many cheers from the men themselves. It was therefore doubly necessary for the officers to maintain the confidence of their soldiers and an anecdote, popular within the army and retold with delight by Macdonald, confirmed that the commander of the 2nd Sudanese had little need to worry about his men's loyalty. At the height of one of

Macdonald's official portrait (BBC Hulton Picture Library).

Young Hector (right) with his family (National Library of Scotland).

Draper's apprentice in Inverness, aged sixteen (National Library of Scotland).

*Gordon Highlanders in action during Afghanistan campaign, 1879 (The
Illustrated London News).*

Captured Afghan guns in the cantonment at Sherpur (National Army Museum).

Majuba Hill: the last act as the British troops retreat (The Illustrated London News).

Edinburgh Castle from the Grassmarket showing the Victorian barracks (Edinburgh City Libraries).

Gordon Highlanders on parade, Edinburgh Castle esplanade (National Library of Scotland).

Macdonald (right) in the Sudan with a fellow officer and N.C.O. of the 1st Brigade.

Omdurman: the Dervish charge on the British lines (The Illustrated London News).

Omdurman: aerial view with Macdonald's 1st Brigade on the right of the British lines (National Army Museum).

the battles along the frontier, probably at Toski, Macdonald roared his orders at his men, anxious to be heard above the noise of gunfire. Mistaking his wrath for anxiety or fear, his men began to crowd around him and to stroke his legs, saying, "Don't be afraid, we are here and we shall protect you. Have no fear it is all right."

On the 25th February 1890 Macdonald received the D.S.O. for his services at that battle and in the following year, on 8th July, he was gazetted major and he transferred his commission from the Gordons to a larger, London-based regiment, the Royal Fusiliers. Because there were no vacancies in the Gordons he was forced to take his substantive promotion in a regiment that he was destined never to serve in or to lead in battle. But having reached his majority, the watershed in any ambitious officer's career, he stood poised for further advancement and his achievements had been well recognised in the dispatches of his superiors, including those of Colonel Kitchener.

Omdurman

Although Kitchener's appointment as Sirdar in 1892 had caused a sensation in Egypt, disgust gradually turned to grudging admiration as he turned his undoubted talents to the total reorganisation of the Egyptian army. A bad commander in the field he may have proved himself to be, but Kitchener was possessed of a methodical mind and he was a good administrator who was well able to act as a catalyst for the 'boys' under his command. Although he was later to earn the anger of his subordinates for his cold-blooded attitude towards the Egyptian, Sudanese and British troops in his army, in those early years in Egypt he quickly won the respect and confidence of his commanders for his cool professionalism and for his ability to interpret the logistics of the Sudan.

His work was aided by the fact that he was responsible to the Foreign Office and not to the War Office, thus avoiding the scorn and possible antagonism of those officers on the general staff who cared little for his rapid rise to power in Egypt. The return of Salisbury's Tory government in 1895 was also a bonus, for it was that new administration, with its avowed policy of promoting pride in imperial achievement, that was to give him the go-ahead for the gradual reconquest of the Sudan. After all, having assailed Gladstone for his inaction on that score, they could hardly refuse to move once the reins of power were in their own hands. Two further events of importance helped him: the first was the publication of Sir Alfred Milner's *England in Egypt* (1895), a propagandist (though by no means inelegantly written) book which promoted the benefits that had accrued to Egypt and her people under British rule, and which also pooh-poohed the Liberal's refusal to reoccupy the Sudan. Pride in achievement and devotion to duty, ran Milner's argument, brought peace and civilisation to where once reigned strife and primitive chaos. Egypt under Milner's boss, Lord Cromer, became almost a personal despotism, modernised perhaps, but completely in Britain's pocket. Of his charge, Cromer was able to say, "The Egyptians should be permitted to govern themselves after the fashion in which Europeans think they ought to be governed,"[1] meaning that self-government was not within reach, and it was with good reason that he was known in Cairo as 'Le Grand Ours'. The second element in Kitchener's favour was the smug and slightly hysterical interest in the Empire that was captivating British society in the year before Queen Victoria's Diamond Jubilee. Alfred Harmondsworth had taken over the *Daily Mail* and had turned it into an unashamed vehicle for Imperial propaganda—"the Daily Mail stands for the power, supremacy and greatness of the British Empire", ran its advertising slogan. Writers too—like Kipling, Haggard and Henley—took up the theme and suddenly wars in far-off places became the ideal place for character building. Tommy Atkins began to be popular folk hero, and Kipling's *Barrackroom Ballads* became something of a bestseller.

In September 1896 Macdonald was promoted brevet-lieutenant-colonel and put in command of the 2nd Sudanese Brigade for the invasion of Dongola province—a move which was seen by Kitchener as the necessary first step in the overthrow of the Khalifa's power in the Sudan. In his brigade, which came to be known as Macdonald's Black Brigade, were the four best Sudanese battalions, the 9th, 11th, 12th and 13th, all of which had gained invaluable service fighting along the frontier, and as G.W. Steevens reported, they made an impressive sight: " . . . fine as are many of our British regiments, these made them look very small . . . however old the black may be, he has the curious faculty of always looking about eighteen; only when you thrust your eyes right in his face do you notice that he is a wrinkled great-grandfather of eighty. But he always stands as straight as a lance. Not that the 9th average that age, I take it, or if they do, it does not matter. Their height must average easily over six feet. They are willowy in figure, and their legs run to spindle-shanks, almost ridiculously; yet as they formed up on parade, they moved not only with the scope that comes from length of limb, but the snap of self-controlled strength as well."[2]

However misguided Steevens might have been about relative ages, he was right about the men of the 9th battalion who were included in Macdonald's brigade, and it was Kitchener who ordered that 'Mac'— as he called him—should bear the brunt of the advance and during the early engagements Macdonald had special command of the native infantry.

Two means of transport suggested themselves to the Sirdar for the moving of his great army south and he made good use of both. It was routine to go by river steamer down the Nile as far as the first cataract, but thereafter it was impossible for those ungainly boats to negotiate the treacherous narrows and hidden rocks of a river that suddenly changed its character and became impassable unless its level of water was high enough. Those steamers were run by the enterprising travel agents Thomas Cook and Son, who controlled the monopoly of public transport on the Nile, and the Egyptian army was obliged to pay for its services on the first stage of their long journey south. So well known was the firm's managing director, John Mason Cook, that when Lord Cromer was visiting a local dignatory he received the gracious, though perhaps unexpected reply that the emir was pleased "to meet any friend of Mr Cook".

From Wadi Halfa at the first cataract there remained the long march across the desert to Berber from which the assault on Khartoum could be mounted. In spite of his lack of concern for his men's welfare and safety, Kitchener was tactician enough to know that an exhausted army, harried by recalcitrant desert tribesmen, could not be expected to fight a pitched battle after long marches over a hot and pitiless desert, and he was aware, too, that the Nubian desert offered some of the roughest terrain known to man. Something more rapid and direct was required and so Kitchener commissioned the construction of a railway across that inhospitable land, a railway that the experts said could never be built, or, if safely constructed, then at terrible cost to human life. As it was, Kitchener accomplished the one goal without the accompanying fatalities and his success was due to his engineer, Edouard Girouard, the son of a distinguished Canadian High Court judge and an expert on the iron road. One of Kitchener's 'boys', he owed his position as much to his expertise as to his charm and good looks: he was one of the few members of the inner circle able to laugh at Kitchener's moods and to be able to influence his chief. It was by dint of hard work and sweat, though, that Girouard built his railway across the desert. Lacking proper finance or equipment, he had to make do with local labour, most of whom did not even know what a railway was, let alone what it looked like, but he had, too, a handful of mildly eccentric, though undoubtedly resilient officers of the Royal Engineers. After the line was eventually built, engines and rolling stock were scrounged from all over Africa and many of them were veritable museum pieces. Of one of the locomotives, Kitchener is supposed to have answered the driver's assertion, that it was unserviceable because of a faulty boiler that might explode, with the words, "That engine could pull a lot of supplies across the desert. We aren't particular to a man or two."

Also included in Kitchener's great army were a number of Nile gunboats of the *Zafir* class which had been built to his own design and which were like toys to an excited child, his very own pride and joy. They were brought in sections to Kosheh on the Nile and built hurriedly in a makeshift yard. Their role was to deny the Dervish army access to the river and to enfilade any position that had to be taken, and as it turned out, with their Maxim guns and naval ten-pounders they were to prove a useful adjunct to the field force. A good indication of Kitchener's almost adolescent ability to indulge in a fit of the sulks and of his belief in perfection only, can be seen in an anecdote related by Sir Philip Magnus. When the first *Zafir* had been completed Kitchener ordered its commander to take it down river to show it off to the troops, but no sooner had she slipped her moorings than a loud explosion ripped through her engine room. She had blown a cylinder. "By God, Colville," said Kitchener to her commander, "I don't know which one of us it's hardest luck on—you or me!"[3] For the rest of the day Kitchener was inconsolable and stayed aboard the cabin of another gunboat, his pride dented, and worst of all, the incident had all taken place in front of an expectant army who thought that the Sirdar could do no wrong.

The first battle—it deserved more the title of skirmish, even though dispatches were written and a clasp struck—took place at the town of Firket where Macdonald's brigade showed its ability again, on this occasion by flushing out the Dervishes from the surrounding hills, and that battle taught the British officers that their men would stand and fight even the most determined enemy onslaught. Kitchener's army lost 20 killed and 84 wounded for over 800 dead and twice that amount wounded or captured. The British Maxim guns took a dreadful toll on the Dervishes, many of whom were still clad for battle as if taking part in a medieval crusade rather than in a modern war. At home, the victory was a cause of much satisfaction and public opinion was instrumental in forcing the Foreign Office to allow Kitchener to complete the occupation of Dongola province.

During this phase of the war, Macdonald's brigade accepted fruitful employment along the lines of communication and by clearing up unexpected pockets of resistance. The earlier years of training through drill and discipline had done their work and by the beginning of the second part of the campaign in 1897 Kitchener was in no two minds that he would have to rely heavily on the Sudanese of the 2nd Brigade. It was testimony to Macdonald and to his leadership and the loyalty it aroused that the Sudanese continued fighting at all. Not only were they taking on an enemy who feared not death, but the Egyptian commissariat's decision to skimp on the quality of equipment and uniforms was beginning to have its repercussions on the troops, whose boots had been made from incorrectly cured leather and contained an insole which rubbed feet mercilessly, rather like the action of emery paper. Despite those discomforts, they continued to march for Macdonald Bey, and their commander, remembering no doubt, what it was like to be a squaddie on the line of march, would dismount from his charger when his men's spirits were low, and take up position on foot at the head of the column. It was at that time that the myth grew up about the attempted assassination and Macdonald's handling of it (see pp. 15-16).

Having received permission from the Foreign Office to proceed farther down the Nile, Kitchener dispatched a column under General Hunter to the town of Abu Hamed and in the ensuing rout of the Dervishes the 2nd Brigade again saw most of the fighting. The next objective was the town of Berber which was taken on the 31st August without encountering any serious opposition and Kitchener, astonished by his own success, suddenly found himself caught on the horns of a dilemma. He had fought his way so far south that if he was to advance again it would only lead to confrontation with the Khalifa but in spite of his thundering successes he realised that to ensure complete victory he would have to rely on reinforcements in the shape of British forces. They might bring with them, though, officers superior in rank to him and he was not at all anxious to see his glory whisked away from him at the moment of victory. Indecision overtook him and to add to this personal misfortune his static army was stricken with an outbreak of malaria and cholera. His anguish was ended by the dramatic news his intelligence staff was able to give him towards the end of the year.

It seemed that the Khalifa was more than a little astonished by the invasion of his country by foreign infidels. Although skirmishing along the frontier had been commonplace for the past ten years or more, he did not relish all-out war and the gradual encroachment of the Sudan alarmed his sense of security especially when news began to filter back to him that the foreign devils were prepared now to stand firm in the face of the Dervish onslaught. Then a dream came to him, a potent dream that told him of victory on the hills of Kerreri near Omdurman, so instead of riding out in force to attack Kitchener's extended army, he contented himself with sending an army of 16,000 led by his emir Mahmud to recapture Berber. If the attack succeeded, well and good; if it failed, then a potentially troublesome lieutenant would be removed from court, and in any case, the Khalifa still had at his disposal a large and committed army.

What the dream did not tell the Khalifa was that the Egyptian army, as Kitchener wished, had been strengthened by a British brigade, whose commander, General Gatacre, would be subordinate to the

Sirdar, and this brigade included three line infantry regiments all with a chilling ability to fire rapidly and steadfastly at an approaching enemy. Having taken the decision to invade the Sudan, Salisbury's administration was determined that failure would not be on the agenda. Thus, the beginning of 1898 saw a large Anglo-Egyptian force camped near Berber at an encampment on the Atbara, a tributary of the Nile. Back in Omdurman, the Khalifa watched events with interest as Mahmud's army was joined by that of Osman Digna—within their *zeriba*, or fortified encampment, his leaders began to quarrel about the correct tactics to use against the infidels camped opposite them. Their arguments were silenced on the morning of 8th April when the British artillary opened fire on the *zeriba*, inflicting massive damage and a huge loss of life on the Dervish army. Kitchener then gave the order to advance on a broad front, the British brigade on the left and Macdonald's in the centre. It was hardly the most subtle of moves and in the withering fire that greeted the advancing columns, Gatacre's brigade, especially the men of the Cameron Highlanders, experienced heavy casualties in the eventual victory. Militarily, the action was effective, the way south now lay wide open, but it was won at much loss of life and added weight to the feeling amongst senior officers that in the last analysis, Kitchener was a bad leader of men in the field, however much he tried to make amends in his dispatches home which went out of their way to give praise where praise was due.

> I fully confirm General Hunter's remarks on the valuable services of the three brigadiers commanding the infantry brigades, viz., Lieutenant-Colonel Maxwell, Brevet Lieutenant-Colonel Lewis and Brevet Lieutenant-Colonel Macdonald. They handled their troops with precision, leading them gallantly in action, and they have shown themselves fully qualified as commanders of troops in the field.[4]

A distressing feature of the victory was Kitchener's treatment of his vanquished foe, the Emir Mahmud. A proud handsome man, who could find no answer to his repeated questions to the British about the reason for their invasion, he was put in chains and led in triumph behind Kitchener during the official marchpast through the town of Berber. Alongside the Sirdar rode Colonel Macdonald and behind them marched the 2nd Brigade on whom Kitchener had accorded the singular honour of leading the formal entry of the town. A raucous medley of music blared from the bands attached to the parade: Highland marches on the pipes and drums, and a mixture of ragtime, music hall and native tunes from the motley collection of brass bands. If it was an image of British imperial power at its zenith, it was also an image that could have sprung from any history book, the Romans leading their slaves in triumph before the Capitol. It was an image, too, in which lay the first signs of that Empire's self-destruction.

What could have been Macdonald's thoughts? An officer for only seventeen years, could he have been so far removed from his origins as to see in the spectacle only the trappings of military glory, the triumph of duty and devotion over sensibility and common humanity, the victory of the strong and virtuous over the weak and wicked? Compassion he may have felt for his own black brigade— honorary British soldiers for the duration of the war—but Macdonald, like his fellow officers, seems not to have been excited by the massacre of Dervishes and the indignities forced upon their leaders. Had he been, then the whole fabric of British power would have been threatened. (This is not to say that Mahmud was a sea-green incorruptible. The Khalifa's rule was oppressive and dominated by an almost medieval use of torture, and massacres of opposing tribesmen were rife.)

The victory on the Atbara ended the spring offensive and many officers were granted leave in Cairo and luckier ones, farther afield; but Macdonald chose to stay on in Berber as the officer commanding. There was time for some shooting and fishing on the Nile and crocodiles became the object of much sport but the summer was long, hot and boring. A brothel was opened in the town but such was the call on its services that an outbreak of venereal disease threatened to incapacitate one of the newly arrived English regiments and it had to be closed.

By the middle of August the army was ready to advance. In Gatacre's British division, General Wauchope, a patrician Scot who grew to know Macdonald well, commanded the 1st Brigade while in Hunter's Egyptian division, Macdonald himself commanded the newly assigned 1st Sudanese Brigade. There were three regiments of cavalry including the 21st Lancers, the only British regular cavalry regiment never to have won a battle honour. Wags had it that the regimental motto was 'Thou shalt not kill'. They were in the Sudan determined to see action, to do or die, and their petulant, thrusting attitude was a bane to the Sirdar. Although those officers, drawn mainly from the landed gentry, were brave to a fault, they were also indubitably bone-headed, reckless and possessed of as little intelligence as was necessary for a gentleman concerned only with the pleasures of the hunt or the gambling table. To their number was added a young war correspondent called Winston Churchill who made no secret of the contempt he felt for his boorish fellow officers, but who was also anxious to see some action and could use the influence of his father, Lord Randolph Churchill, to make sure his wishes were fulfilled. (And fulfilled they were. He took part in the 21st's nonsensical charge against the Dervishes on the morning of Omdurman.) He was under contract to the *Morning Post* and his book, *The River War*, is one of the best accounts of the war in the Sudan.

Churchill was one of sixteen war correspondents who had taken their places as 'honorary officers' in the allied army and they were a mixed bunch. Amongst their number were the experienced Bennet Burleigh, G.W. Steevens and Fred Villiers (of the *Illustrated London News*) but they also included a querulous Oxford don, and the *Manchester Guardian* was represented by a schoolmaster whose only qualification was that he was a rowing Blue. Kitchener loathed them, whatever their experience, and did his best to make life difficult for them. Shortly before Omdurman he kept the press corps waiting outside his tent in the hot sun before emerging and pushing them out of the way with the angry words, "Get out of my way, you drunken swabs!"[5] It was a mistake, because the press was taking a good deal of interest in the campaign which had aroused so much excitement in a Britain approaching the heights of jingoistic fervour. Kitchener was to make many enemies on account of his handling of the press.

Macdonald, on the other hand, adopted a different attitude. "Colonel Macdonald treated us to the luxuries of the use of his bathtub, soap and towels, and then gave us a splendid breakfast, and later on lunch, the first good meals we had since quitting Wadi Halfa", reported Burleigh[6] during the march south, and on another occasion when he arrived with a colleague to interview Macdonald he was met with the words, "Never mind about all that, what are you going to have to drink?"[7] It was the beginning of a friendship between the two men that was to last over the coming five years and beyond, and the Glasgow-born Burleigh was to espouse the cause of his fellow countrymen with an ardour that went beyond national sycophancy: he was one of the many correspondents, including Steevens and Churchill, who were to believe that Fighting Mac was given less than his due for his actions in the Sudan and later during the Boer War.

The army, which had grown to include, 8,200 British troops, 17,600 Sudanese and Egyptians, 44 field guns and 20 Maxims (plus 36 naval guns and 24 Maxims on the gun boats), a large contingent of cavalry and camel corps, together with all the necessary camp followers, made its sedate way south to Atbara where it was forced to spend a few idle days before embarking on the river boats that would take them downriver to the plain near the Kerreri hills where they would do battle with the Khalifa and his Dervishes. At that point

Kitchener brought into service a strange force of 'friendlies', made up of irregular tribesmen, hostile to the Khalifa, and deserters from his army, whose task it was to guard the east bank of the Nile and to prepare the artillery positions for the bombardment of Omdurman. Their commander was a noted Arabist and scholar, a Lawrence of Arabia before his time, called Major, the Hon. Edward Montagu-Stuart-Wortley. This mild-mannered eccentric had become a close associate of Macdonald's through their mutual interest in Arabic (which Macdonald had mastered at an early stage) and he was to stand by his friend later when all around were loosening their grips on prior friendship. Like Macdonald he enjoyed the complete trust of his men, but his force was surely one of the weirdest to have fought under a British flag; their weapons were relics from the crusades, or at best eighteenth-century in origin, and their 'friendliness' could depend on the outcome of the battle.

The river boats took the rest of the army to Wad Hamed and ahead of them lay the penultimate stretch: the fifty-odd miles to Omdurman, the Khalifa's mean city, more of an elongated village but made divine through the siting of the Mahdi's tomb in its centre, a shrine that could not be surrendered, ever. There, the Khalifa kept within the realms of his dream, believing that victory would be his on the plains outside the town, beneath the frowning Kerreri ridge. Logic told him that he was only required to wait behind his defences, to allow the infidels to exhaust themselves beneath the hot desert sun, before rushing forth to deliver the blow of the divinely just. But that deceptive logic knew nothing of the power of lyddite and the range of the British howitzers.

On the morning of 1st September the gunboats and the artillery opened up a fierce barrage on Omdurman. Not only did the falling shells cause terrible carnage and damage but the gunners had been taking bets on who could score the first hit on the Mahdi's tomb. Soon the range was found and to the consternation of those inhabitants who believed in the supremacy of Allah over modern science, the tomb received a number of direct hits. "The man-killing effects were very good," observed one laconic British officer, "and I am told the moral effect also was very great." Given so much confusion in his camp, the Khalifa was forced to agree with his emirs that the only path to victory was to engage the infidels on their chosen site of battle, which happily compared well with that dreamt by their leader—on a bend in the River Nile beneath the ridge of the Kerreri Hills.

Kitchener had drawn his up troops in a wide arc with the river behind him and the gunboats ready to give covering fire. On the right, to the north, was Macdonald's brigade which included two experienced battalion commanders, Major Charles Fergusson of Kilkerran of the Grenadier Guards and Lieutenant-Colonel Smith-Dorrien, both of whom were to play important roles, as was Fighting Mac's A.D.C., Lieutenant Pritchard of the Royal Engineers. Maxwell's 2nd Egyptian Brigade was next in line, flanked on the left by Wauchope's and Lyttleton's British Brigades who were to bear the brunt of the first attack. When it came at 6.30 a.m. it presented an awe-inspiring spectacle: line after seemingly irresistible line of Dervishes made their way forward in tight battle order, a wave of humanity pressing on to break on the concentrated fire of the British and Egyptian infantry. And through the cool morning air came the chants of the devout. *"La llaha illa llah wa Muhammad rasul ullah"* ("there is but one God and Muhammad is the messenger of God").

Many of the British and Egyptian battalions had armed with dum-dum bullets to give their Lee-Enfields greater carrying (and killing) power and as the Dervish charge on its broad front continued, the battle began to take on the aspect of a slaughter. Pounded by howitzer shells, riddled by the Maxim and scythed down by the steady hail of bullets, the Dervish army, urged on by its emirs, charged to certain death. "They came very fast," reported Steevens, "and they came very straight, and they presently came no further."[8] When the excitement of that first charge died down and the cordite smoke cleared, some 2,000 Dervishes lay dead in front of the British lines and many, many more broken bodies were left to crawl painfully away from the field of carnage. The massacre was almost over and it was only 9.00a.m.

Macdonald's hour, and his chance to gain a place in the index of history's pages, was still to come and it had its origins in the Sirdar's decision to press on to take Omdurman. As the great army lined up to swing south, Macdonald's brigade was left to bring up the rear without a friend in sight and with an expanse of hostile ground between it and the main army which was in jubilant mood. Macdonald's unfortunate position was exploited by a large group of Dervishes including the Khalifa's choice troops, which had regrouped behind the hill of Jebel Surgham. It was an ideal place from which to start an attack and the emirs waited until the British brigades, eager to win the right to enter Omdurman first, were beyond retrieval, before they exhorted their men afresh to disregard life and to find their places in Paradise. It was a dire moment for the British, one that could have lost the newly-won victory and Macdonald was aware of the danger. Pritchard was sent galloping to the Sirdar with the news of this new threat but received the dusty reply that Macdonald was not to engage but to continue his march on Omdurman. Had that order reached him and had it been possible to execute Macdonald would no doubt have carried it out, but he was already under fire, and before Pritchard could gallop back, the sound of gunfire from the north could be heard ringing across the plain. "Hello. That must be Mac!" said Kitchener and immediately made preparations to move Maxwell's brigade to Jebel Surgham to cover Macdonald's flank.

Back at Macdonald's lines, Steevens and Burleigh had been quick to spot the site of the next piece of action and Steevens reported that Fighting Mac, "very gleeful in his usual grim way", had welcomed the journalists to their vantage point and had promised them "some good sport". Macdonald had been kicked on the knee by a fellow officer's horse and was in considerable pain, but once his blood was up nothing could withstand him or his men. The sight of the approaching Dervishes had worked up the Sudanese into a frenzy and they were blasting off their rifles without thought of aim, or more importantly, of ammunition. Confusion reigned as the air became loud with rapid gunfire, screams and curses, as the Sudanese fired for all they were worth. Alive to the danger, Macdonald grabbed Pritchard and walked out in front of his men, knocking up their rifles with his swagger stick. The ploy worked and as the Dervishes, the pick of the Khalifa's army, approached Macdonald's lines, they met not unsustained shooting but a withering curtain of rapid fire that had them reeling. It was a brilliant example of controlled discipline, carried out under the most dangerous and terrifying circumstances and the Sudanese' courage was equal to the task. But no sooner had that attack been repelled than a fresh danger faced Macdonald.

A Camel Corps' officer arrived at Macdonald's lines with the news that a new and formidable force, numbering perhaps 20,000 was about to hit him from the north. Surely the time had come to withdraw but when General Hunter's A.D.C. galloped up with that very order, Macdonald, doubtless showing again that same grim jollity, replied simply, "I'll no do it. I'll see them damned first. We maun just fight."[9] What happened next was the wonder of all who saw it. Macdonald called his commanders together and hurriedly sketched out in the sand his plan of defence. The battalions were to move one by one into a new line of battle and, beginning with the 11th, that is what they did, Macdonald even managing to find the time and energy to berate those who did it out of sequence. To have accomplished that complicated manoeuvre on a parade ground would have tried even the hardest veteran but to have executed it under a barrage of heavy fire was a demonstration of leadership and controlled discipline at its best. And perhaps it was only a man like

Macdonald, steeped in the lore of drilling, who could have carried it out. Later, everyone was to be wildly enthusiastic, even though at the time it must have been seen as a move combining the foolhardy with the optimistic.

But the cockpit of the fight of Macdonald's. The British might avenge his brigade: it was his to keep it and to kill off the attack. To meet it he turned his front through a complete half-circle, facing successively south, west, and north. Every tactician in the army was delirious in his praise; the ignorant correspondent was content to watch the man and his blacks. [wrote G.W. Steevens] 'Cool as on parade,' is an old phrase; Macdonald Bey was very much cooler. Beneath the strong, square-hewn face, you could tell that the brain was working as if packed in ice. He sat stolid on his horse, and bent his black brows towards the green flag and the Remingtons. Then he turned to a galloper with an order, and cantered easily up to a battalion commander. Magically the rifles hushed, the stinging powder smoke wisped away, and the companies were rapidly threading back and forward, round and round, in and out, as if it were a figure in a dance. In two minutes the brigade was together again in a new place. The field in front was hastening towards us in a whitey-brown cloud of Dervishes. An order! Macdonald's jaws gripped and hardened as the flame spirited out again, and the whitey-brown cloud quivered and stood still. He saw everything; knew what to do; how to do it; did it. At the 'Fire' he was ever brooding watchfully behind his firing line; at the 'Cease fire' he was instantly in front of it: all saw him, and knew that they were being nursed to triumph.[10]

Having wheeled his brigade, Macdonald then had the task of meeting that last fanatical attack, and at one point, as wave after wave of Dervishes ran to certain death, it seemed as if their suicidal tactics might win the day. On some parts of the front the Sudanese were engaged in fierce hand-to-hand fighting, their ammunition having finally been exhausted and the 10th were already taking the brunt of the onslaught with fixed bayonets. "The valiant blacks," reported Churchill, "prepared themselves with delight to meet the shock, notwithstanding the overwhelming numbers of the enemy."[11] At that point the Lincolnshire Regiment hove into view and their rapid fire—they were supposed to be the most efficient sharpshooters in the British army—soon dispersed the Dervish ranks and the enemy began to retire to the safety of the Kerreri hills.

The battle was over and the Anglo-Egyptian lines secure but even though Kitchener was to remark as he watched the Sudanese giving chase to the Dervishes, "I think we've given them a good dusting gentlemen!" he had little cause for satisfaction. Defeat had almost been snatched from the jaws of victory and through his own tactical stupidity he had placed Macdonald's brigade in a position of the utmost danger. He might have been credited with the victory as Sirdar, but everyone in his army with an ounce of sense to rub together agreed with Burleigh as to the real victor.

> Beyond all else the double honours of the day had been won by Colonel Macdonald and his Khedivial brigade, and that without any help that need be weighed against the glory of the single-handed triumph. He achieved the victory entirely off his own back, so to speak, proving himself a tactician and a soldier, as well as what he has long been known to be: the bravest of the brave. I but repeat the expressions in everybody's mouth who saw the wonderful way in which he snatched success from what looked like certain disaster. The army has a hero and a thorough soldier in Macdonald, and if the public want either, they need seek no further. I know that the Sirdar and his staff fully recognised the nature of the service he rendered. A noncombatant general officer who witnessed the scene declared that one might see 500 battles and never such another able handling of men in presence of an enemy. [12]

10

Scotia's Darling

The sight that met the victors on the road to the town of Omdurman was that of the charnel house. Bodies, broken by the artillery, lay in pools of anguish, their broken limbs and spilled intestines grim testimony to the efficiency of the barrage of high velocity shells. Some of the wounded betrayed the helpless stoicism of those about to die in the cause of the righteous, others decided to take an infidel or two with them before departing this life, and the advancing British army was often obliged to kill or be killed as wounded Dervishes made final despairing attacks on their ranks. Those no doubt necessary measures gave rise to stories of British atrocities against the wounded and Winston Churchill who harboured no love for Kitchener was quick to place the blame on the Sirdar and his lack of feeling for the fallen. "I shall merely say," he wrote to his mother, "that the victory at Omdurman was disgraced by the inhuman slaughter of the wounded and that Kitchener was responsible for this."[1] The truth of the matter, if it can ever be deduced, was that Kitchener probably turned a blind eye to the actions of his men. His Sudanese troops hated the Dervishes with a missionary fervour and once their blood had been heated by the fury of battle, it was difficult to calm them down, and there were always British soldiers ready to follow their example.

Then the race was on for the glory of entering Omdurman first and it was the 10th Sudanese who claimed that right, not so much *du meilleur rang* as by thrusting through the British ranks and brooking no opposition, even from the stately Grenadier Guards who found Sudanese bullets whistling over their heads when they stood their ground. Then came the Seaforths who had captured the Khalifa's black flag and in their midst as they marched into the slum that was Omdurman, rode Kitchener on his white charger, in his own mind at least the equal of any Khalifa. As they made their way through the dirty streets the soldiers must have wondered why they had come so far to win so little—a collection of sprawling shacks with poor, round-eyed inhabitants, some already beginning to suffer from the worst effects of starvation. It was hardly a scene from the *Arabian Nights*. At the Mahdi's tomb, Smith-Dorrien led in his 13th Brigade to deliver the final indignity: the desecration by infidels of a place sacred to those who worshipped Allah the most merciful. It was perhaps at that point, with the Khalifa long fled into the desert's wastes that the people of Omdurman realised that they were well and truly beaten.

The victory at Omdurman was hailed in faraway Britain and the success of British arms was greeted with applause throughout the Empire. (Only a handful of radicals and intellectuals, including Wilfred Scawen Blunt, greeted the news with derision and feelings of outrage.) But it had been not so much a battle as a massacre, the triumph of the Maxim gun and the dum-dum bullet over the chainmail, swords and muskets of another age. To be sure, the *Pax Britannica* had been extended along the Nile and another country appeared red on the atlas—today there is red of a different hue at Omdurman, on the ridge of the hill of Jebel Surgham, which overlooked Macdonald's finest hour, stands a Soviet radar station— but many of the Anglo-Egyptian force questioned if it had been worth while, the long journey over weary miles, to avenge one man.

Having praised the Lord on the following day and given him thanks for helping the Sirdar to avenge Gordon, Kitchener proceeded to demonstrate the superiority of his god to the Khalifa's. The Mahdi's grave was razed to the ground and his bones, with the exception of his skull, were tossed into the Nile. Kitchener decided to keep the stately skull and would have had it mounted in silver for use as a drinking cup, but the story was leaked to the press and in the ensuing furore he had the skull buried quietly in the Moslem cemetery at Wadi Halfa.

However, not even that hiccup could prevent Kitchener's reputation from taking a knock. His luxuriant moustache became the symbol of all that was supposed to be good and virile about the Empire and his features appeared everywhere, on biscuit tins, tea caddies, buttons, trays, postcards, wherever there was space. Every schoolboy knew of his feats and there was tremendous public excitement when it was announced that he had been awarded a peerage, taking the title Kitchener of Khartoum, £30,000 and the thanks of both houses of parliament. Other officers also received due reward. Macdonald was made a C.B., promoted full colonel and appointed aide-de-camp to Queen Victoria. He too received the thanks of both houses of parliament and a modest cash award, but there were men like Bennet Burleigh who felt that those were meagre pickings for a man who had accomplished so much.

The 'Highland Toast' to Macdonald in the Hotel Cecil, 6th May 1899
(The Illustrated London News).

Highland revenge: Fighting Mac appointed to South Africa, January 1900.

Paardeberg: defeat into victory (National Army Museum).

Macdonald (second left) and fellow generals during Boer War (Scottish National Portrait Gallery).

Field Marshal Lord Roberts of Kandahar, Pretoria, 23rd October 1900 (BBC Hulton Picture Library).

Macdonald in the uniform of an aide de camp to Queen Victoria (BBC Hulton Picture Library)

Kitchener of Khartoum with his A.D.C. 'Brat' Maxwell (BBC Hulton Picture Library).

William Macdonald.

Lady Macdonald and her son Hector Duncan.

Ceylon: planters' picnic with elephant (National Army Museum).

Field-Marshal August von Mackensen leaving church in Bucharest, Christmas Day 1916 (Imperial War Museum).

Von Mackensen: the family portrait.

*Von Mackensen photographed in 1918
(National Library of Scotland).*

*Sketch of Macdonald's funeral in the Dean Cemetery (The Illustrated
London News).*

Colonel Hector A. Macdonald alone seems as yet to have had extended to him scant military recognition of his invaluable services. The post of A.D.C. to Her Majesty is a coveted dignity, but a mere honorary office, carrying neither pay nor emolument. Indeed it is the other way, for the accessories required to bedeck the person will cost at least £25.[2]

He went on to say that the people of Scotland, particularly of the Highlands were indignant about the treatment meted out to their hero and "pertinently ask if the authorities wish no more Highland recruits". It was a call that was to be heard again at the conclusion of the Boer War, and the Scots who are quicker than most to perceive an insult, real or imagined, began to believe that Macdonald had enemies in high places and that it was Kitchener who stood between him and promotion.

And so arose a belief that Fighting Mac was being victimised because of his Scottishness, his low-born origins and his lack of connections. Apologists pointed to the fact that it was he who had been the true hero of Omdurman and that he had been most unfairly treated by an ungrateful government. Kitchener was the obvious scapegoat but there is no evidence in his papers at the Public Record Office that he disliked Macdonald or indeed at the moment of victory that he was jealous of his subordinate's success. On the contrary, his personal writings on the battle were warm in Macdonald's praise and his official dispatch makes generous mention of 'Mac's' part in the battle.

Macdonald's brigade was highly tested, bearing the brunt of two severe attacks delivered at very short intervals from different directions, and I am sure it must be of greatest satisfaction to Colonel Macdonald, as it is to myself and the whole army, that the very great care he has for so long devoted to the training of his brigade has proved so effectual, enabling his men to behave with the greatest steadiness under most trying circumstances, and repelling most successfully two determined Dervish onslaughts.

Part of the problem was that the expedition had been carried out under the direction of the Foreign Office through Lord Cromer in Cairo and it was to them that Kitchener reported; in those exalted circles Macdonald enjoyed no influence whatsoever. While matters rested in the hands of Whitehall, there was little hope that Macdonald would receive very much in the way of public honours, for the time being, at least.

Macdonald stayed with the army of Egypt until the Spring of 1899 when he bade farewell to the men of the 1st Sudanese Brigade and returned home to a well-deserved period of leave. Even if he had not received the knighthood that many thought was his due, the public took him, somewhat hysterically, to their hearts and he was lionised everywhere he went in Scotland—people rushed forward, anxious to clasp the hand of 'Fighting Mac', the embodiment of British pluck and determination. The *Highland News* of the 13th May 1899 summed up the feelings of Macdonald's fellow countrymen in an editorial written to coincide with his triumphal return to the north: "What was thought to be wanting in the acknowledgement of the authorities, his countrymen at home, were resolved, as far as they were able, to make up, and this week they have shown in a most remarkable manner their warm appreciation of their countryman's conduct in the hour of trial and peril."

Macdonald's first public honour, and the first of many banquets, was held in London, at the Hotel Cecil on the evening of 6th May. It had been arranged by the joint Highland Societies of London and the Duke of Atholl presided over a glittering assembly of around six hundred guests including representatives of the Scottish nobility, the House of Commons and the army, notably by Macdonald's commander from the Transvaal, Sir Evelyn Wood. Even the diminutive figure of J.M. Barrie was there, to record his fatuous observation on the occasion that there was "the sound of the bagpipes" about so many fine-sounding names. Speeches were made in Macdonald's praise and he was presented with a magnificent sword of honour which had been crafted by the Company of Goldsmiths and Silversmiths of London. Although it was a througly pleasing evening for all concerned, there was a touch of farce in the sumptuous Highland costumes worn by many of the guests, peacock finery that owed more to romantic notions about the Highlands than to the realities of living there. Many spoke Gaelic who refused to speak it at home in Scotland and when the order was given for a 'Highland toast', the waiters were astonished to see the guests stand up with one foot on the table to drink Macdonald's health. And to complete the evening it broke in a sea of sentiment and praise for Scotland in the worst possible taste but quite in keeping with the spirit of the age.

> Excepting Mr William Allan M.P. for Gateshead not one of the following speakers caught the ear of the audience, though among them were such and so competent men as Lord Kingsburgh, Lord Strathcona, the Earl of Dunmore, The Macintosh, Sir David Tennant, Agent-General for the Cape, and Sir Horace Tozer, Agent-General for

Queensland. Mr Allan said it was "a gran' nicht for Scotland, the best since Bannockburn", and he found favour at once. He touched the spot. Parliament was only a show run by Scotsmen. England was run by Scotsmen. What would the world be without Scotsmen—without US (with much emphasis). We are the salt of the earth, and so on. Mr Allan acted the part well. His broad chest swelled visibly. He spoke as a man having conviction and a mission to impress humanity with it. His patriarchal beard and flowing locks grew greater and longer and more imposing with the eloquence, and he finished in a blaze of patriotism.

That report from the *North Star* of Dingwall a few days later was typical of the kind of breathless journalism that accompanied the reports of the many meetings of people anxious to bask in Macdonald's reflected glory. When the haggis was borne in, piped in by the men of the Black Watch, the *North Star's* reporter could not repress his sense of pride. It was as if in later days, Scotland had not only won the World Cup but had thrashed England in so doing. Behind the pipers, limped an "array of plantigrade Cockney waiters feeling frightfully out of place and oblivious to the honour of their position in being privileged to bear on high Auld Scotia's fare—great chieftain of his race. It was, however, most amusing."

Later, Macdonald was to admit that he wished he had the price of the sword of honour in his pocket but his reply to the speeches that evening betrayed no emotion, only the modesty that came to be associated with his utterances at public occasions. A contemporary of Macdonald's , James Milne, was at the banquet and his description of the man was to become well-known in the weeks that followed as Macdonald received the praise and thanks of his fellow countrymen. "He is broad of chest, but if ever he puts on all his medals and orders there will not be much room to spare. The whole figure is shapely, sinewy—the kind of framework that the mind governing it can take anywhere and do anything with. It has grace, distinction, all those attributes which you mean when you speak of style. In actual stature he is not, perhaps, more than five feet ten inches."[4] Other writers were to make much of the idea that Macdonald was a simple son of the soil, whose head had not been turned by the honours heaped upon him, and a man whose trappings of success sat uneasily upon the fighting soldier he had become. The photographs of him taken at this time show the conventionally posed portrait of a soldier, proud of his uniform and his sturdy military bearing, though there is a curious gentleness, too, in his eyes.

He began to be concerned that the publicity surrounding his name would damage his military career and he begged friends to make little of his success. Society took him up and Lady Jeune, mother-in-law to St John Broderick, Secretary of State for War, became a patron; he dined at Windsor with Queen Victoria and left her his signed photograph; in Scotland the landed gentry vied with each other to entertain him, little suspecting that their lonely bachelor had a wife and child in Bedford, whom he hardly ever saw. Just as Robert Burns kept quiet about Jean Armour while he was being lionised by Edinburgh society in an earlier century so also did Hector Macdonald maintain his own counsel about his private life.

His next move was to Glasgow where he was entertained to luncheon by the corporation and in the evening he attended a concert in his honour in the Bank Restaurant given by the Gordon Highlanders' Association and was given the opportunity of meeting men who had fought with him in Afghanistan and at Majuba. There, too, he was presented with a sword of honour, in the style of a claymore, by the Clan Macdonald Society of Glasgow in an act of generosity that was to have a curious sequel. A year after its presentation an article in the *Daily Mail* of 4th September headlined, 'When Scot meets Scot', alleged that the sword was a fake, worth only £7 instead of the £250 given to the jeweller who made the sword, C.C. Macdonald of Duke Street, Glasgow. The implication was that the money had been embezzled and that Hector's sword had snapped in two while he carried it with him on active service in South Africa. In fact, that statement was true: part of the hilt had been broken when someone had tried to force the lock of its case during transit, but the jewellers angrily refuted the charges in a specially printed pamphlet and in February 1901 they successfully sued the *Daily Mail* and won both an apology and damages for £750. Later, the same paper was to report that Macdonalds were "conducting as brisk and snug a business as one could desire". Another, less controversial honour given to him in Glasgow was the award of an honorary LL.D. by the University of Glasgow in recognition of his services in the Sudan.

It was in the north, though, that the public praise was to reach its highest as the towns of Inverness-shire and Easter Ross competed with each other to put on the most magnificent display. Perhaps the proudest of these was at Dingwall where he received the freedom of the burgh on the 11th May. He was met at the station by Sir Kenneth Mackenzie of Conan, Lord Lieutenant of the county, and taken to a flower and banner bedecked Dingwall where five thousand of his fellow countrymen thronged the streets to welcome the hero to his home county. After the presentations of an address of welcome and his burgess ticket, Macdonald made his customary short speech of thanks, ending with words that were to become more serious and pointed as the tour wore on. "I wish you to understand that it was only by sheer hard work and duty that I have been enabled to come here today to receive your warm greetings and I should wish to impress upon the youth I now see before me that that is the only way to get on in this world." And after the ceremony, at the National Hotel where he was the guest of his old employers, the Robertsons, he gathered a group of youngsters around him and gave them a message that he was to repeat several times during his leave in Scotland. "Now boys, as there are no reporters here, I will give you a speech all to yourselves. That speech is—Be good boys, join the Volunteers or army, and don't forget your parents, Queen and country!"[5] Two days later, in Tain, he repeated the message, after receiving the thanks of the town council, and added that he thought the time had come for Britain to have a large standing army made up of men who would serve the colours for a period before returning again to civilian life as fully trained soldiers. In other words, Macdonald was an early advocate of national service, and as we shall see later, his promotion of that theory was to cost him friends in high places.

But during that summer of 1899 the War Office was nothing loath to see Fighting Mac receive such hysterical praise from the Highland towns. He had, in effect, become the army's finest recruiting sergeant and his presence in Scotland did wonders for the army's conscription figures. Everywhere, in fact, people were anxious to hold up the example of Hector Macdonald as all that was good in the ideals of service, discipline and duty. Speaking to the boys of the Duke of York's Military School, Lord Wolseley said that the days were long gone when social position and inherited wealth determined a soldier's future. "In the Khartoum campaign, amongst those who led Her Majesty's and the Egyptian troops was one whose name had now become a household name, not only in Scotland where he was born, but in every part of the Queen's dominions."[6]

The profession of arms, in Scotland at least, had undergone a sea-change following the victories in the Sudan. Two famous Highland regiments, the Camerons and the Seaforths, had fought at Omdurman and on the North-West Frontier in India in 1897, the Gordons had again distinguished themselves under the fire of hidden tribesmen desperately defending their territory against the encroaching tentacles of the British Empire. This new feeling of pride in 'Jock' was to stand the Empire in good stead during the Boer War which was only months away and when Scottish casualties, by Edwardian standards, were to be exceptionally high. The Gordons were to lose 132 dead and 384 wounded at Magersfontein, but they were also to fight in more engagements and win more medals than any other regiment: six Victoria Crosses, ten Distinguished Service Orders and thirty-two Distinguished Conduct Medals. And the fervour refused to die down by the time the First World War began. In August 1914, the Royal Scots Greys and the Gordons were amongst the first regiments to land in France and the first territorial battalion to see active service on the western front was the London Scottish Regiment. By then it was not always unemployment that had taken men away to join the colours—more often it was the powerful attraction of the myth of the bravery and steadfastness of the Highland regiments, a myth that had been created partially by the career of Fighting Mac. (Even to this day, new recruits to the Gordons are told his story and reminded that they too can follow his example.)

After the Highland tour Macdonald visited Aberdeen, where it had all begun twenty-nine years earlier. He had always maintained a warm affection for the city and carried with affection the memory of the welcome given to him as a raw recruit—in the King Street barracks, where the Gordons maintained a depot, there were still old quarter-master sergeants with vivid memories of young Hector. In Inverness he met Sergeant Pocock who had given him his first rudimentary instructions in the art of drilling; Edinburgh gave him the freedom of the city; but the warmest welcome, perhaps, came from the people of Mulbuie, on a rain-soaked day when he met many of his old friends in the schoolhouse at the road end near the now prosperous croft of Rootfield. To the great disappointment of the crowd he was in mufti but his modesty and lack of side were remarked upon: the Scots are very quick to bring down climbing hypocrisy and to puncture vain aspiration. It was therefore noted with grim approval that when his old dominie, Alexander Treasurer, asked him what it felt like to be in the heat of battle, Macdonald replied, "I don't think you feel anything in particular."

At the summer's end the junketing and the fêting, and the country house weekends, came to an end too and Macdonald returned to London where he put up at the Army and Navy Club before leaving to take up a new command in India. Earlier on, during his leave, it had been decided that he was to move to India as commander of the Sirhind district with the local rank of Brigadier-General. Although Sirhind was designated in the Army List as a second-class command, the district included the huge cantonment at Simla where amongst the regiments responsible to him was to be the 2nd battalion Gordon Highlanders. The wheel had come full circle for there were still officers in the regiment who remembered Macdonald as a young subaltern.

Macdonald left for India on the 24th October 1899, a fortnight after the Boer War had broken out, and his friends noticed the disappointment he felt on not being re-assigned to a war command. Having enjoyed fifteen years of seniority in the Sudan, it was a bitter pill to swallow to revert to the British Army Lists and to take his chances of promotion along with the next man. It was also true that being an infantryman told against him, as the majority of the leading commanders in the war were to be cavalry men and that fact was to be a source of much rancour when Macdonald eventually arrived in South Africa the following year.

But all that lay ahead of him in the last restless years of his life. On the evening of his departure for India his leave ended as it had begun, with a ceremonial dinner. His hosts were the London branch of the Gordon Highlanders' Association and the other principal guest was their colonel-in-chief, the Prince of Wales who offered the toast to Macdonald, "Success to him, and may he live for many years."

11

Fighting Mac!

Fighting Mac's appointment to the Sirhind district in India was seen in Scotland as a just, if belated, reward for a soldier who had served his country so well. *The Scotsman* newspaper reported the news with an air of smugness and went on to compare him with an earlier Scottish soldier who had risen equally dramatically from obscurity to a position of public authority. "It was the proud boast of the late Lord Napier of Magdala that he landed in India a poor subaltern of Engineers, with nothing but his sword, and that he subsequently rose to be local commander in chief; but it will be a prouder boast for Colonel Macdonald if he is able to say, as he very probably will, that he has fought over the same ground as a Sergeant of Highlanders and as a General of a division."

But the general who arrived in the Sirhind district was not the same soldier who had fought with such careless rapture in the Sudan. The long months of socialising in Britain had placed a great strain on his reserves: it was one thing to face up to the onslaught of 20,000 Dervishes, but quite another to spend idle weekends amongst gushing hostesses anxious to make something of this shy retiring man. Not that he was rude. His letters of this period betray a quiet charm even when turning down invitations as he had to on the 18th July 1899 in a letter to Lady Munro of Foulis whose son he had offered to help.

> Please say in what way I may be of use to your son. The thing is, what does he want and is he in any way qualified. Many thanks for reminding me that I was to visit you in the North. I am afraid, however, that I shall have to go off to India very soon in which case I shall not have the pleasure of renewing our acquaintance.

Never one for society, he must have hated the idleness of long empty days (his only privacy during his leave came at his aunt's house at Ardochy near Inverness); warfare had been his only coinage for three decades and peacetime soldiering, with its necessary social round, suited him ill. "You had only to mention her name at afternoon teas for every woman in the room to rise up and call her not blessed," said Rudyard Kipling of Mrs Hauksbee, his fictional doyenne of Simla society. "She was clever, witty, brilliant and sparkling beyond most of her kind; but possessed of many devils of malice and mischievousness."[1] Faced with 'devils' of that kind, Macdonald kept within the safety of his headquarters at Umballa where he sat in the Sirhind Club "fighting battles with matches and working himself into a state of irritation". That *Daily Sketch* report was written after Macdonald's death but there is little doubt that during his two-month stay in India he was in a state of acute depression. One of the reasons for this state of anxiety, which manifested itself in jumpy, irritable, tense behaviour and a restless desire for action or distraction, was that he was in need of rest—his leave in Britain had not provided that—and the general's tension began to tell on his subordinates as he became a sullen and unapproachable martinet.

There may have been other more tangible medical grounds for his anxious state of mind. During the latter stages of the Sudan campaign he had been stricken with malaria and although he had managed to throw off the worst of the disease, it is known that the long-term effects of severe bouts of malaria in sub-tropical climates can cause depression, and he was never one to face up to the medical facts of life, as a popular anecdote told after Omdurman illustrates—a medical officer who suggested that Macdonald rest because he was in the grip of a fever and high temperature, was promptly threatened with arrest.

His anger had also been nourished by his failure to win a command in South Africa in the Boer War that had broken out on 11th October. Like most of Queen Victoria's wars it was a continuation of a previously unresolved conflict in which British pride—in this case the defeat at Majuba—was still thought by many to be at stake, but this war was to be a very different affair and the most protracted full-scale conflict involving Britain since the Napoleonic campaigns. It was to cost much in terms of manpower and resources and as a precursor to what was to happen later in the century, Britain's large volunteer army was to lose many men, often needlessly. As usual, it began with disaster for Britain. When Kruger ordered the British to withdraw from the Transvaal, the ultimatum that led to war, Britain had only a smallish force in South Africa but even its strengthening under the command of the redoubtable Sir Redvers Buller could not compensate for the idiotic way in which the British had forgotten the lessons of 1881.

During all the early battles, the British insisted on advancing on a broad front towards the hidden Boers who were content to pick off the advancing enemy before retiring to fight another day. The British high command may have raged against such 'ungentlemanly' conduct but their own methods played right into the hands of an enemy who believed in fighting a fast-moving campaign in the open spaces and mountains of their homeland. The nadir of muddle-headed thinking came on the night and early morning of the 10th and 11th December when the Highland Brigade—comprising the Black Watch, Argyll and Sutherland Highlanders, the Seaforths and the Highland Light Infantry—was ordered to sweep the Boers from their position in the Magersfontein hills above the Modder River. Lord Methuen, a general who "exhibited considerable bravery, but few brains"[2] had command of the army entrusted with the relief of Kimberley and his tactics to move the Boers had an ominous ring to them, particularly in hindsight to those who were to fight again in Europe in fourteen years time. Because the Boers had entrenched themselves on the hillside with barbed wire in front of them Methuen decided to order his artillery to bombard the positions before making a frontal attack. Thirty-one guns opened up on the evening of 10th December and the men of the Highland Brigade stood transfixed by the display of modern gunfire as high velocity shells tore into the hillside showering rocks and scrub into the clear air. Surely no one could survive in such a holocaust, but the Boers, forewarned of the British intentions, had decamped to the other side of the hill where they waited in comparative safety. Only three of their number were wounded. But not only were the Boers out of danger—they now knew to expect a British attack.

The Highland Brigade was commanded by General Andy Wauchope, a popular Black Watch officer whose first military service had been in the Royal Navy. The laird of Niddrie in Edinburgh and a landlord made wealthy from the revenues of coalmines on his property, Wauchope was extremely popular within the army and had even gained a political reputation in 1892 by standing against Gladstone in Midlothian and making a dent in his majority. In the Sudan he had commanded a British brigade at Omdurman and had become a friend and admirer of Fighting Mac's—next to him Wauchope was one of the best known Scots in the British army. It was his task to lead the Highlanders by night towards the Boer lines but in the pitch darkness with a thunderstorm rolling overhead and lightning flashing all around them, the quarter columns of the four regiments became confused and they advanced too far. As the grey dawn broke Wauchope tried to deploy his tired men but was prevented from seeing the order carried out by rapid and accurate fire from the Boer lines which tore through the Highland ranks. In almost the first fusilade Wauchope was killed instantly and panic began to seize the closely packed companies of men.

Advance was impossible due to the Boers' defensive measures, which included the use of barbed wire, and retreat became the only imperative for the leading companies as men fell dying in the maelstrom of fire from a hidden enemy. Discipline failed as men began to mill around the slopes of the hill; some men tried to run, others took what cover was available to them, but for the most part, the Highlanders were forced to remain where they were, pinned down by the hail of bullets that flew all around them. A company of Seaforths broke through the Boer line and could have saved the day but their nerve failed them when seven hidden Boers, including one of their leaders Pieter Cronje, opened up a sustained fire on the hundred-odd British troops. The Argylls' courage was restored when their Pipe-Major struck up the regimental march 'The Campbells are Coming' and, when the Gordons arrived to add some much needed backbone, there was good reason for optimism. But by the day's end the dispirited brigade began to retire, and not always in good order, from the scene of their ignominious defeat.

> Then I saw a sight I hope I may never see again [wrote an observer, Roger Poore]: men of the Highland Brigade running for all they were worth, others cowering under bushes, behind the guns, some lying under their blankets, officers running about with revolvers threatening to shoot them, urging on some, kicking on others; staff officers galloping about giving incoherent and impracticable orders.[3]

As the battle drew to its inevitable conclusion Methuen ordered up the King's Own Yorkshire Light Infantry and the Scots Guards to steady the line as the kilted Highlanders made their inglorious retreat from the hillside where over seven hundred of their number lay dead.

In Scotland the news of the defeat was met with disbelief. On the streets of Edinburgh women wept openly and social occasions were hurriedly cancelled; but there was a sense of shame too that such a distinguished group of Scottish regiments should have been forced to flee the field of battle in front of their English and Welsh comrades. No one blamed Wauchope for his faulty judgement, instead fingers were pointed at an English inefficiency that had sent so many brave lads to an unnecessary death. The same week—"black week", as war correspondent Arthur Conan Doyle called it—dragged on with further setbacks at Stormberg and Colenso and an angry British press began to mount a campaign for Lord Roberts to take over command in South Africa. Their wishes were granted in January 1900 when he arrived at Cape Town with his second-in-command Lord Kitchener of Khartoum. On the 4th January satisfaction was completed by the appointment of Hector Macdonald to the command of the Highland Brigade. His long wait was over and when he arrived at the Modder River twenty days later to take over the unhappy, badly mauled brigade, word quickly spread that the Jocks had a new commander in Fighting Mac. And just as the war correspondents in the Sudan had taken him to their hearts so did they too in South Africa where Arthur Conan Doyle, another fellow Scot, was to become a particular admirer.

> A bony, craggy Aberdonian, with a square fighting head and a bulldog jaw, he had conquered the exclusiveness and routine of British service by the same dogged qualities which made him formidable to Dervish and to Boer. With a cool brain, a steady nerve, and a proud heart, he is an ideal leader of infantry, and those who saw him manoeuvre his brigade at Omdurman speak of it as the one great memory which they carried back from the engagement. On the field of battle he turns to the speech of his childhood, the jagged, rasping, homely words which brace the nerves of the northern soldier. This was the man who had come from India to take the place of poor Wauchope, and to put fresh heart into the gallant but sorely stricken brigade.[4]

Macdonald could see that there was little point in instilling a sense of discipline in his men. They possessed that and only required to find it again. And so after briefing his brigade commanders he went out amongst the men and let them see that he meant to get to know as many as was possible in the short space of time available to him before he led them again in action. He was also adamant that the Brigade should regain its honour in Scottish eyes and a series of letters to prominent people underlined the importance he placed on its performance in the field. "You will I am sure be pleased to learn (after the aspersions cast on the Brigade about Magersfontein)," he wrote to the Provost of Glasgow on 27th February, "that I am perfectly happy with the work done by them, now in action twice under my eyes—work which perhaps none but themselves could have done half so creditably." The actions referred to were Koodoosberg and Paardeberg, neither famous encounters but both helped the Highland Brigade to recover its lost nerve. And in a letter to one of his erstwhile hostesses, Mrs Macleod of Cadboll, dated 3rd March he told her with pride that "the Highland Brigade lacked none of the qualities which made them so famous in former campaigns and that I am very proud indeed of being in command of such men". Another letter, to the Clan Macdonald Society, thanking them for his clansmen's congratulations, assured them of his "duty to see that neither the army nor the Clan will suffer in name through me". Macdonald, like other senior officers, kept up a varied correspondence with several youngsters (Kitchener was particularly close to Lord Desborough's son, Julian Grenfell who was to become one of the Great War poets and to die on the Western Front) and one of the letters that has survived was written to a Glenalmond schoolboy, Alister Robertson, the son of an Aberdeen doctor with Gordons' connections. Although its familiar tone may make odd reading today, there is little doubt that it was composed in the spirit of service to an Empire that Macdonald hoped would never change. "Many thanks for the photographs which I like very much. Can you guess why I like the small one best? I am sending you a tin of the Queen's chocolate which you can eat with your best friends and think of me. You should keep the tin as a memento." After describing the boredom of waiting for battle, the letter ends, "And now for a lecture for not giving me more news in detail. News, news, news! to please me—all about your own dear self."

The Highland Brigade's first skirmish under Macdonald took place on the morning of 7th February when he was ordered to hold the hill at Koodoosberg Drift, but although his men did well to draw the Boers on to the level ground on top of the hill, the hidden sniper fire began to tell heavily on the Brigade and they were ordered to retire. The position Macdonald had found himself in was similiar to that occupied by Colley at Majuba and although he was loath to retreat, discretion must have told him that it was madness to risk the safety of the Highlanders so soon after their recent mauling. Newspaper reports of the time—and the Boer War not only occupied most of the daily news space in the popular press but also spawned numerous illustrated magazines—expressed their disappointment at Macdonald's less than successful manoeuvre and an Irish Nationalist M.P. asked derisively in the House of Commons, "Has Fighting Mac been beaten?" It was not a question designed to appeal to the Scottish members and The Times reported that "the Highlands will not forget it". The real reason why Macdonald was not given the opportunity to shine in the war was partly because the nature of warfare was changing rapidly from the set-piece battles to which he had become accustomed in the Sudan, and also because Roberts was unwilling to risk using his infantry in great numbers. Mobility and good management became the names of the British tactics and those who would not conform were sacked. In the wake of Roberts's arrival, five generals, including Gatacre, and six brigadiers, were relieved of their commands.

Roberts's successes continued in the early part of 1900 with the relief of Kimberley and a victory at Paardeberg during which Cronje and 4,000 Boers were captured. It was an undistinguished battle and Kitchener's first victory in South Africa—he had assumed command while Roberts was convalescing—and it proved yet again that, however much he might have been respected as a tactician and administrator, Kitchener was an indecisive leader of men. The Highland Brigade, having marched 31 miles in twenty-four hours, with the men carrying "100 rounds of ammunition, besides his greatcoat, cholera belt, one day's ration, bottle of water, waterproof sheet and blanket, the whole weighing something like 60 lbs", [5] was ordered to make a frontal attack on the Boer lines and they found themselves, as at Magersfontein, pinned down beneath accurate rifle fire. Smith-Dorrien's 19th Brigade became bogged down in the swollen Modder River before making a dramatic charge into the murderous Boer gunfire. By the end of the day there were 1,262 British casualties including Hector Macdonald who had been shot from his charger, 'Knowall', while making a reconnaissance with his A.D.C. Captain Wigham. In a letter to Mrs Macleod of Cadboll he explained that "the bullet entered the outside of my left foot, just under the ankle joint and came out at the other side a little lower down—a very clean wound, which if caused by a Martini bullet, would have cost me my foot." [6]

Lord Roberts arrived at Paardeberg the following day, 19th February, and immediately forbade Kitchener to waste more lives in unnecessary infantry assaults. Instead, the Boer laager was pounded into submission by heavy artillery fire and on the morning of 27th February, the nineteenth anniversary of Majuba, Cronje and his army surrendered to the British. Although the Boer plight had been desperate for at least a week, Roberts was determined that they should be made to hold out until it could be said that Majuba had been wiped from the slate. As The Times reported the following day, the suggestion had come from Macdonald who had "sent from his bed a note to Lord Roberts reminding him that Tuesday was the anniversary of that disaster which, we all remembered, he had by example, order and threat, himself, done his best to avert, even while the panic had been at its height".

Macdonald was not present at the surrender and was forced to stay in hospital until the 10th March. Typically, stories began to filter through the Highland Brigade to the rest of the army about Fighting Mac's stubbornness. A field hospital orderly, Private Maclennan, told

the press that Macdonald had spurned the offer of a place of safety
and had cursed the orderlies to "please hurry and bind up my foot;
I've got lots of work to do out there yet". Another story told of his
stern discipline that "not infrequently makes a sacrifice of popularity", as had been the case with Lord Kitchener in the eyes of "his
loudmouthed detractors". During the course of the battle of
Paardeberg, Macdonald had come across some malingerers hiding
behind a kopje and his response to their plight was not one of comm-
iseration. "Now, ye darrety hounds," he exclaimed in a tone of
withering scorn, at the same time drawing his revolver and tapping
his right palm with it, "ye darrety hounds, ye know what I should like
to do with ye. Now git on, I say, git on, ye darrety hounds." [7] It was a
new mood and, during the course of 1900, one that was to be
remarked upon by British officers who had always looked on
Macdonald as being a mild-mannered disciplinarian.

His wound, though not serious, took a long time to heal and it
effectively ended his war in South Africa. Again, his mental state
could have affected his physical condition. The euphoria he had felt
on taking over the Highland Brigade had disappeared in the
aftermath of his wound and a feeling of paranoia began to creep into
his correspondence. To his brother William he wrote on 30th March a
desperate letter forbidding him to speak to the press. "I notice in
several papers a garbled story of my wound, purporting to have been
supplied by you. Of course I know such was not supplied you. But in
case of accidents, I wish you to remember what I wrote to you some
years since, not to give any information concerning me to the
newspapers. Do please try to bear this in mind." And it is noticeable
in press reports at that time that William did, indeed, do his best to
disassociate himself from the mild hysteria that followed the news of
the wounding of so popular a soldier—one paper even reported in
sombre tones that 'Knowall', Macdonald's charger, "was killed on the
day the distinguished general was taken to the Hospital. A Boer shell
did the deed." One report, in an anonymously published news-sheet
helped to defuse the situation by poking fun at the press's insatiable
appetite for news from the South African front.

MACDONALD'S WOUND
Monday morning: "Macdonald only received a single wound; but,
being in the ankle it is painful."
Monday mid-day: "Macdonald's single wound is not troublesome, as it
is only in the little finger."

Monday evening: "Macdonald's single wound, being in the lungs, causes much anxiety."

Tuesday morning: "Macdonald's single wound—in the hip—is doing well."

Tuesday mid-day: "Macdonald's single wound—which penetrates the brain and lives and ends at the great toe—is somewhat painful."

Tuesday evening: Macdonald's single wound causes no uneasiness, as it is only in the haversack."[8]

The wound—which would have caused some pain—continued to trouble Macdonald throughout the summer and in a letter of 30th August to a friend of the family in Ross-shire, he referred to it as "a good foot still, though it pains me occasionally with the changes of weather and when I place it on a stone in walking or begin dancing a Highland fling, and perhaps I would not back it to tire in a 30 mile walk!" It added to his feeling of depression, too; he became irritable and short-tempered and it only required a minor upset for an already short fuse to blow. When a volunteer battalion arrived at Bloemfontein to strengthen his brigade the men were tired and dishevelled after a long march but instead of the expected words of welcome from their new commanding officer they were given a sound ticking-off and told to clean up their uniforms without a moment's delay. And on another occasion he angrily berated a cavalry unit for their slovenly riding and threatened to take away their mounts there and then[9]. To Kitchener he wrote despairing letters about the uselessness he felt in being so in-active and he spoke of his own "Profound helplessness"[10] and pressed his doubts about the efficiency of the British Lee Enfield rifle.

The Highland Brigade had been ordered out of the front after Paardeberg to take up the unrewarding, though extremely necessary task of guarding the British lines of communication and this new duty made Macdonald feel more keenly his own lack of involvement in the war. Some of his theories about the administration of the war were reported in the press and they would not have been calculated to win him friends. He refused cavalry support because he doubted that the horsemen could keep up with his infantrymen. With regard to intelligence about the enemy's movements, he suggested that it would make more sense, as he had done himself, to bribe the Boer children with sweets, to discover their fathers' whereabouts. An admirer of the government troops who had fought against the confederates in the American Civil War, Macdonald claimed that they were better soldiers because they refused to bow to traditions or to notions of dignity. Then he returned to his favourite theme: that of conscription. In a letter to the *St James Gazette* of 14th March he stated that the South African war had only strengthened and confirmed his ideas. "I should take the period for service just after a man has finished his apprenticeship, or been a short time a journeyman, but not yet settled down. A year or two at that period, in an age ranging from 21 to 23 would not, I am convinced, injure one's prospects if passed in a well-regulated army, and a well-regulated army a conscript army is bound to be."

Other officers, including Kitchener, were sceptical about Macdonald's theories and pointed to the tremendous support Britain had received from volunteers from all over the Empire. Macdonald remained adamant, though, that a British army would only remain a professional instrument if it relied on trained conscripts who would be well paid and well looked after by the military authorities who could in turn rely on their services in time of war. His ideas gained a wide currency and for a man so averse to the press he showed an uncommon ability to use journalists to propagate his own ideas. Some of his theories were incorporated in Haldane's reforms of 1907 when an army reserve was established, but in 1900, during wartime, many felt that it was wrong of Macdonald to air his views and to gain publicity from them.

Towards the end of that year Macdonald moved with his brigade to Aliwal North, a pivotal town on the Orange River and an important railhead. There he came into contact with the scores of refugees who were then beginning to mill around the country in the wake of the warfare. One of the worst concentration camps had been established near the town and it fell to Macdonald's men, amongst their many other duties, to guard it. It was a distasteful task. When the British had established the camps they had given no thought either to the logistics of providing food and shelter for large numbers of people or to the emotional grief caused to those who had been uprooted from their homes. An attempt to bring order to the chaos caused by the refugee problem they might have been, but like any camp surrounded by guards, they were inhuman and degrading. Many of the Scots in the Highland Brigade had a sneaking regard for the Boers—one sergeant had told Macdonald that "It's an awfu' thing to fight against such a God-fearing people"—and consequently the Highlanders were welcomed when they arrived at Aliwal North, as a letter from a Boer prisoner of war to the *Invergordon Times* of 10th October 1900 testified: "General Macdonald, whom we all admire, as all men should, went up to my home when passing through Frankfort. He is most amiable and kind-hearted. He took delight in enquiring after the welfare of others, and my wife assures him that the Tommies were not troublesome." Macdonald was in fact one of

the few British generals to take an interest in the Boers and their way
of life, and it was remembered by the Boers later that he saved an old
farmer's belongings by signing a note that all would recognise. It read
simply "Don't interfere with these cows—Hector Macdonald."[11]

His interest in the welfare of the Boers was also to cause him much
grief later for it was at Aliwal North that he was rumoured to have
had a homosexual relationship with a Boer prisoner. Both Roberts
and Kitchener mention it in their papers[12], but like the other charges
that were to be brought against him, nothing exists about them in the
official records. No one had noticed any tendency towards
homosexual behaviour in the Sudan and even though the officers in
the Sudanese army had been suspected by many of indulging a taste
for buggery (see p77) there were so many British in the country in
the way of soldiers, administrators, observers and the press, that any
behaviour that did not smack of the conventional Victorian code of
morality, would have been remarked upon. It has been said by
Macdonald's apologists that the rumours were started by those who
were jealous of his popularity, but while that may be so, it should be
said that by the beginning of 1901 Macdonald was in a sorry
predicament, far removed from the central action of the war, and like
a caged lion, keeping himself very much to himself. In a tent that was
"neatness itself, no outward show at all, nothing but what was useful
(wrote the war correspondent T.P. O'Connor) and everything in its
place, the only hint of colour introduced being a curtain of varied
Oriental colours", Macdonald would hold court and speak in a
"delightfully indiscreet" way about how the war was being run, and
about the reasons for his inactivity.

To a private soldier who had brought him a bottle of malt whisky
from the Royal Atheneum Hotel in Aberdeen he insisted on offering
a dram, saying that although he had been teetotal for a time, good
whisky should not be left undrunk. He spent more and more time
with his men and became increasingly cut off from the officers in
high command, a new generation with new ideas who were starting
to see in Macdonald a tired old man with tired old theories. Roberts
returned to England in January 1901, leaving Kitchener in supreme
command, and the new boss was in no mood to keep on his sulking
subordinate. At the beginning of April, the Highland Brigade was
disbanded and Macdonald was relieved of his command. In a
telegram to Roberts he suggested that Fighting Mac should be
allowed to return to India. The reply from Roberts shows a degree of
surprise at the turn of events but it was obvious that Kitchener had to
be allowed to do as he thought fit. "Macdonald can return to India
whenever you like. I rather hoped he would have chosen to stay in

South Africa, but as he has a lien on the Indian appointment, he can, of course, return to it."[13]

Despite the fact that Macdonald seemed to have had a say in his future, much was made about his precipitate departure from South Africa and Kitchener was again cast as the villain of the piece. But by then Macdonald was probably not in a fit state to take a new command, even assuming that there was one there for him: it made sense to give him a rest—other officers, including General Sir Archibald Hunter, accepted the same fate with little fuss. When the question of his having been 'sacked' from South Africa was raised in the House of Commons, the government's reply that he was "destined to rise yet" was fair comment in the circumstances. Like an express train gradually running out of steam and in need of refuelling, he slid gently into the siding that the government had prepared for him. He returned to London on the S.S. *Carisbrooke Castle* in April 1901 and was knighted by King Edward VII on the 14th May. That night he dined with Lord Roberts who had become chief of the Imperial General Staff and perhaps the most influential and best-loved soldier Britain had ever had; then, a week later he was off to India, on the P&O overland route through Paris and Marseilles to take up the command of the Southern District army at Belgaum in India. Those were hardly the rewards of an officer who had fallen completely out of favour with his superiors.

12

Pro Consul

Before leaving for India, Macdonald wrote to William apologising for his inability to come north; and to reporters who had tried to pin him down on his new appointment he showed a nice sense of tact in evading all their questions. The press had to be content with a few anodine remarks on his plans for the future and with a bare description of the man they saw off at Victoria station: "He was in a suit of tweeds, a light overcoat and a cap. Judging by the four little pieces of luggage—a tin dispatch box and three bags marked H.A. Macdonald—the famous leader of the Scotch Brigade believes in travelling light."

Macdonald arrived in Madras in late June to take up his appointment at the cantonment of Belgaum but it was not long before the old doubts returned. In order to take up the Indian appointment without delay, he had forfeited three months' leave and he began to feel that the future could not be faced without a change of ambience. To Roberts he sent a number of telegrams putting his case for leave of absence; Roberts consulted the King and in the autumn it was decided that Macdonald should pay an official visit to Australia and New Zealand. Although it was classed as "privilege leave" in the official records, it was in effect a flag-raising tour designed to drum up support for Britain amongst the people of two of her most stalwart dominions and to ensure that Australasian soldiers would always be on hand to answer the Empire's call, as they had done so readily in South Africa.

A long and demanding programme of speeches, receptions and official dinners was arranged for the general and his visit proved to be an immediate success, so much so that by the end of October *The Times* was suggesting that Macdonald might be offered the post of commander-in-chief of the Australian army. "In such a position he would not be trammelled and restricted as he has too frequently been in the past. There are indeed few military appointments involving such wide discretionary powers and the sense of independence would be particularly grateful to a soldier who, possessed of great ability, naturally longs for the opportunity of putting his ideas into practice." As it was, the appointment was not offered to him and in War Office circles it was rumoured that it was his very 'ideas' on military matters that had cost him the promotion.

Throughout the Australasian trip he kept returning to the themes of conscription and the training of youth for a career of service to arms. On 12th October in the Caledonian Club in Melbourne he spoke approvingly of "Australia's wise plan to provide all cadets with a uniform, to insist on discipline, and to ensure, as far as possible, that cadets on leaving the school joined in other branches of the defence system." In Adelaide he ended his speech by saying that "If what he had said would induce any father to devote his boys to the service of their country, he would consider that his visit to this land had not been without some results." To a reporter of the *Sydney Sunday Times* of 17th November he expanded on his ideas. Every boy would receive mild military training while at school and at the age of twenty-two would enlist for a period of six to twelve months with further periods of service thereafter. "Wise nations," he said, "prepare, not for the purpose of making war, but to prevent war, and the more thoroughly a nation is prepared to defend itself, the longer it will remain at peace." Then, seizing the opportunity, he went on to criticise the direction of the war in South Africa, returning to his old idea that drill and discipline made the ideal soldier. But as Magersfontein and Paardeberg had made agonisingly plain, courage and the ability to obey orders were not enough in the face of the new guerilla tactics and Macdonald's assertion that the "irregular commandoes could not stand against disciplined troops" was a trifle out of touch with reality.

At home his views were a source of annoyance in radical circles and they were looked on with disquiet by the War Office whose line was that Britain did not need a conscript army then or in the future. But Macdonald had made his mark in Australia and in New Zealand where his carriage was pulled through the streets of Auckland by crowds of cheering ex-patriate Scots. By the end of the visit he admitted to not only feeling better but also to a new confidence in his ability to handle official occasions with their necessary social niceties and speech-making, so much so that the *Melbourne Argus* reported with some suprise Macdonald's new relaxed manner.

> The crowd was beginning to wonder where Sir Hector Macdonald was, when a sturdy thick-set, cheery-looking man, scarcely middle-aged stepped out in a brown slouch hat, soft shirt and a blue sac suit. There

was nothing military about this man. The twinkling eyes of this born
humourist had never looked on the face of death. The spirit of good-
fellowship and geniality that simmered all over his visage was not the
characteristic of the man who had commanded brigades, and welded a
black rabble into a tempered weapon. The Hector Macdonald the
crowd knew was a dour, stern man with a hard, unyielding jaw—the
man whose picture had been published a hundred times—and they
stood aside to let this good-natured contractor or station overseer get
out of the way for the general. Colonel Hoad followed close behind,
and every eye was fixed on the door of the carriage. But instead of
ushering out another passenger Colonel Hoad indicated the thick-set
bronzed humourist with a wave of his hand and announced,
"Gentlemen, this is Sir Hector Macdonald."[1]

By the end of December his leave was up and Macdonald returned
to India to renew his command at Belgaum in January 1902. When he
arrived there the press announced that he had been promoted to the
command of the troops in Ceylon and that he had been elevated to
the post of paid aide-de-camp to King Edward VII. Macdonald's lack
of surprise suggests that he already knew of the appointment to
Ceylon and the official records confirm that view. In a letter of 27th
March 1903, written two days after the suicide, Roberts wrote to
Kitchener claiming that Macdonald "never ceased writing and
telegraphing until I moved him to Ceylon". He preceded the remark
with the hint that there had been "grave suspicions" about
Macdonald's behaviour at Belgaum and that those might have been
the reason for his requesting such an immediate posting. Could those
"grave suspicions" have been homosexual in origin? Nothing exists
on the matter in the official records as none of Macdonald's
dispatches on the subject are in the Roberts Papers and although
Kitchener mentioned the rumours in his reply, it is difficult to
contradict or to confirm Roberts' statement. At home in Scotland it
was believed that Macdonald wanted to place a greater distance
between himself and Kitchener who had just been appointed
commander-in-chief in India. A third reason was financial. The
Ceylon posting would have paid more and was senior in rank to the
command at Belgaum.

The notion that Macdonald was wary of Kitchener does not bear
much examination at this point. Kitchener was not in a position to do
Macdonald any harm, and even though he had in effect asked for
Macdonald's removal from South Africa, as we have seen, he had
every reason for reaching such an unpopular decision. That leaves
the "grave suspicions" and the need for more pay, both of these
pressing enough reasons for the general to request a change of

command. But lack of pay was not the problem that it had been in his early days as an officer. As a major-general and commander of the troops in Ceylon, Macdonald would have been relatively well off, even though he had to meet out of his pay the expense of a house in Dulwich, his son's education at Dulwich College and his own entertaining in Ceylon. That he succeeded to some extent can be seen in the fact that he left his son £4,000 in his will and maintained six accounts in banks in London, Cairo, Bombay and Umballa.

Homosexuality may have been the cause. It was at the root of a good deal of public interest in Victoria's reign despite the fact that repression (pederasty was a capital offence until 1828) made it impossible for homosexuals to exist other than in terms of secrecy and frequent degradation. Even medical opinion tended to believe that it was an illness bordering on insanity. For most homosexual men it became a secret vice, one that either had to be fought by sublimation or marriage, or occasionally relieved through prostitution. Guardsmen from the Chelsea Barracks in London were always game for a spot of 'backgammon' and several brothels in the area traded solely for lonely homosexuals and the young guardsmen they picked up for paid sex. More notorious was the male brothel at 19 Cleveland Street off the Tottenham Court Road which specialised in providing young boys for its clients. In the autumn of 1889 it was raided by police who uncovered a vice-ring run by one Charles Hammond and which included telegraph boys and a number of prominent members of society including Lord Arthur Somerset, son of the Duke of Beaufort and a member of the Prince of Wales's Marlborough House set. And in 1884 Dublin Castle had been racked by a series of homosexual intrigues involving civil servents.

The imprisonment of Oscar Wilde in 1895 following his liaison with Lord Alfred Douglas and the unsuccessful attempt to sue his father the Marquess of Queensberry, was seen by many as the final word in sexual depravity and a witch hunt began for homosexuals in high places, especially in the Liberal Party. Queensberry's eldest son, Viscount Drumlanrig, committed suicide after being accused of having had an affair with the Earl of Rosebery and Frank Harris reported that "Every train to Dover was crowded, every steamer to Calais thronged with members of the aristocratic and leisured classes, who seemed to prefer Paris, or even Nice out of season, to a city like London, where the police might act with unexpected vigour."[2] And also in the wake of the Wilde case the December issue of the *Review of Reviews* stated candidly that "Should everyone found guilty of Oscar Wilde's crime be imprisoned there would be a very surprising emigration from Eton, Harrow, Rugby and Winchester to the jails of

Pentonville and Holloway", for it is clear from contemporary evidence[3] that homosexuality not only flourished in the English public schools of the period but was actively encouraged by many of the masters. In a recent study of contemporary and historical homosexuality in Britain, H. Montgomery Hyde paints a brutal picture of school life at Harrow as remembered by J. Addington Symonds.

> Every boy of good looks had a female nickname, and a boy who yielded his person to an older lover was known as the elder lad's 'bitch' . . .the talk in the dormitories and studies was of the grossest character, with repulsive scenes of onanism, mutual masturbation and obscene orgies of naked boys in bed together. There was no refinement, just animal lust, and it was little wonder that what he saw filled the young Symonds with disgust and loathing.[4]

From the closed community of the public school most boys progressed to the equally cloistered world of the university, the armed services or the church. There they either forgot their childhood experiences or capitalised on them in private—in the late Victorian world there was a certain vogue for camp behaviour, male brothels did a roaring trade and in the twilit world of pornography, homosexual magazines found a ready market. By his upbringing Macdonald did not belong to the public-schooled upper classes but by 1899, if he had wanted to avail himself of them, the delights of the homosexual *demi-monde* were there for the asking. It is certain that he had not betrayed any homosexual or extra-marital heterosexual activity between his commissioning in 1881 and his return to England in 1899—there were too many witnesses who would have no doubt reported anything unfavourable to a man who had risen from the ranks. The incidents at Aliwal North and Belgaum, while not substantiated, could have occurred while his defences were down and in Victorian times even the placing of a hand on another man's knee could be misconstrued, as William Johnson, the Eton master (and composer of the *Eton Boat Song*) had found to his cost in 1872.

Because Macdonald was in a position of authority, any indiscretion, however small, could damage his name and because he knew that his career would always hang on a knife's edge he had to be additionally circumspect. To all intents and purposes he was a bachelor, a man of habit, excluded from the comforts of domestic life and like other Victorian bachelors, such as C.H. Dodgson, Kenneth Grahame and Francis Kilvert who wrote of their experiences, given in his latter days to attacks of 'nerves'. And like Kenneth Grahame, who eventually married and had one son, it is possible that, having comsummated his marriage, Macdonald had decided that sex with a woman was not for him. If he had been a hidden homosexual during his earlier years, the mental strain that he had experienced in India and South Africa, coupled to his newly found time of leisure, may have eased his defences, allowing his natural instincts to take over. A similar fate had met Dr Charles Vaughan, the headmaster of Harrow, who attempted to put an end to homosexual vice in the school through a mixture of the scripture and frequent floggings. In 1858 he himself entered into a sexual relationship with a boy, Alfred Proctor, and the subsequent revelation to a parent forced him to resign his post and to become something of a social outcast—he was also forbidden to take the bishopric of Rochester when an unknowing Palmerston offered it to him. Vaughan was married to the sister of Benjamin Jowett, the Oxford scholar, and he was a noted figure in ecclesiastical circles, yet his one discovered indiscretion ruined his career.

When he landed in Ceylon on 25th March 1902 Macdonald was therefore a man who may have been under suspicion and the governor, Sir Joseph West Ridgeway would in any case have been briefed by the Colonial Office about his new commander, about whom he would have known much already. Ridgeway was then in his fifty-eighth year and after a lifetime of public service in India, Ireland and Russia, he was reaching the height of his career. In 1879 he had been political secretary to General Roberts and had been present in Kabul when Macdonald had received his commission. Ridgeway had been given this undemanding position in 1896 in preparation for his expected retirement from public life: he was not expected to exercise much power in the island, as Ceylon's proper government was in the hands of the Ceylon Civil Service, a lordly organisation composed of well-educated Englishmen who had reached their positions of authority through social position and the passing of rigid Colonial Office examinations. Amongst their number in 1904 was Leonard Woolf, who left a vivid record of his life in Ceylon in the daily diaries he kept until 1911.

> It (the Ceylon Civil Service) was well organised and well disciplined, its members were selected from certain social groups and after selection they were intensively trained for the business of ruling. A strict code of official discipline grew up and it was strictly followed together with an elaborate social code regulating conduct not only among themselves, but between them and other Europeans and the "Ceylonese". The caste sought for and kept power exclusively for themselves.[5]

Although the governor had nominal command of an executive council which was composed of the colonial secretary, the King's advocate, the colonial treasurer, the government agent of the Central Province and the officer commanding the troops; and of the Legislative Council which was the sole law-making authority (in his official position Macdonald was a member of both), effective power lay in the hands of the chief civil servant, the colonial secretary, and his subordinates. Ridgeway was, though, in a position of military authority over Macdonald.

Since 1802 the service had governed the island and during that time Ceylon had evolved its own social codes, centred around the upper class manners of the planters. "Planters nearly always married into one another's families when they returned from their education in England, and they lived a well-ordered country gentry's life. People were normally At Home once each week, and there were frequent calls, and dances at the Queen's in Kandy, and golfing weekends at Nuwara Eiya, and the bungalows were lofty and cool and lapped in lawns, and there was an English vicar at the church up the road, and all seemed changeless, useful and very agreeable."[6] All in all, Ceylon was a tightly-knit community, bound together by a series of interlocking rules and regulations and possessed of a good deal of white self-confidence and superiority. It was not the most ideal habitat for the troubled general who had received a fresh setback when his friend, the soldier and African explorer, Richard Meinertzhagen, had turned down his invitation to accept the post of A.D.C. "I had a letter from Sir Hector Macdonald this evening wishing to know whether I would accept A.D.C. to him whilst he commands in Ceylon. I have wired refusing. I should never care for such an appointment, even if I were not under orders for East Africa."[7] With his social graces and undoubted charm and ability, Meinertzhagen would have been an invaluable asset to Macdonald when he took on the white brahmins of Ceylon society.

Two incidents, in particular, betray his state of mind during his eleven month command in Ceylon. The first occurred when he was asked to present the colours to the Boys Brigade in Colombo. "Now boys," he said in his official speech, "this is by no means the first time I have had the pleasure of inspecting this flourishing brigade, and I have a very lively recollection of inspecting one company of clean-limbed, well-set-up, broad-chested and open-eyed boys, whose discipline, drill, exercises and general manoeuvering forced the applause, time after time, of a vast throng of cultured and critical onlookers." Having praised the brigade for their own skill, Macdonald ended by hoping that when the boys grew up they would transfer their allegiance to the colours, and that they would become "manly fellows, with erect carriage and easy bearing, neat in dress and appearance and glorying in youthful vigour". The speech was well received, expecially amongst the planters who were much impressed by Macdonald's call to the service of Empire. Their illusions were shattered a few weeks later when he inspected the Ceylon Militia—a volunteer force made up, in its officers at least, of white planters and whose Colonel-in-chief was the Governor. "Thoroughly practical, Sir Hector Macdonald came down to the grounds without any ceremony, and taking command himself, he dealt with the whole battalion in the same way a sergeant with a band of recruits. He shouted at one of the officers."[8] The gentlemen of the militia resented being shouted at and being told to tidy up their uniforms and their attitudes to soldiering, especially by a man whose voice suddenly smacked more of the sergeant-major than the major-general. After all, they were gentlemen, not soldiers to be bullied by a jumped-up ranker.

Not surprisingly, Macdonald spurned polite society and turned down invitations to parties and receptions. He did not entertain himself, as occasions of that kind had to be paid out of his own funds and so he spent most of his time immersed in military matters. Later he became friendly with a number of Burgher families—old Ceylonese families of mixed European, usually Portugese, and native Ceylonese origins—who were mainly connected with banking, legal and government interests. Unlike the Eurasian communities of India, the Burghers enjoyed a greater deal of social mobility, being a minority group like the Malays, and even though they were beyond the pale as far as the upper echelons of Ceylon's society were concerned, they were respected members of the community. (Although even a liberal like Leonard Woolf referred to a "dirty Burgher lawyer"[9] in one of his Ceylonese short stories.) Macdonald enjoyed their company, particularly the friendship of a family called de Saram, but just as Kitchener had outraged English society in Cairo by spending his leisure hours with the people whose company he preferred, wealthy and civilised Egyptians, Jews and Turks, so also was Macdonald to pay for his lack of allegiance to the white planter class.

13

"Grave, very grave charges"

The first hint that Macdonald's friendship with the de Saram family would end in grief, came when he began to be suspected of spending too much time with their children, especially with their two sons. Rumours began to take wing in Ceylon that the presents which Macdonald gave to the two boys went beyond the normal bounds of friendship and it was whispered that a sexual relationship existed between the two young brothers and the general. But no evidence survives to prove the stories true and they remain what they always were: rumours.[1] Macdonald was fond of young people: he maintained a correspondence with young Alister Robertson of Glenalmond, and he always made it a point of honour to reply to all his 'fan mail' from youngsters all over the Empire. Then the rumour-mongers pointed to the fact that homosexuality was an accepted and natural fact of life amongst the native Ceylonese. But the de Sarams were a strict Burgher family whose code of morals probably owed more to their Portugese ancestry than to local customs.

When the accusations were made, though, they do appear at first sight to have had some substance to them. According to the relevant Colonial Office Papers[2] West Ridgeway, in his signals to London, referred to a "habitual crime of misbehaviour with several schoolboys", although there is no evidence to prove that the allegations had any foundation in law or whether they owed their existence to the currency of idle gossip. No legal process was ever started, at that time, to arraign Macdonald on specific charges —and that option was open to Ridgeway as he was the general's superior officer with overall command of the British troops on the island. If specific charges of homosexual misconduct had been brought against Macdonald then it would have fallen to Ridgeway to have arrested his officer, commanding the troops, because homo-sexuality was an offence punished by military law. It may not have been a crime under the civilian code of law in Ceylon but its very mention was enough to ruin a British soldier. However, Ridgeway did not take that course of action. Instead, he pondered the matter for some time before confronting Macdonald with the accusations.

As to their nature, two versions exist of what might have happened. The first, told by Lord Tollemache, Ridgeway's grandson, had it that Macdonald "was unfortunately discovered with four native boys in a railway carriage in Kandy. He was surprised by an English tea-planter who immediately recognised him."[3] All would have been well had the planter been discreet, but it was too good an opportunity to miss and when he returned home he told his wife and family what he had seen. Slowly, but surely, Ceylon tittle-tattle found a means of piercing the general's armour and perhaps of ridding their society of what most of them considered to be a vulgar upstart.

The second version, pieced together from Ridgeway's reports and items in the contemporary press, also concerns a train. Seventy schoolboys were to be cited as witnesses and the complaint was to be brought by two clergymen of the Anglican congregation in Kandy. Although actual details are hazy and clouded by prim Victorian obfuscation, it can be deduced that Macdonald exposed himself in a railway carriage that was carrying the boys back to their college in Kandy. While it is hardly a gross offence, exhibitionism, as exposure of the genitals is termed under the law, would, obviously, have been a cause for complaint to the governor. It was not a court martial offence, by any stretch of the imagination, and as exhibition-ism is usually associated with men of weak sexuality or even impotence it does not wear well with Macdonald's psycho-sexual make-up which, as I have suggested, was controlled by a sublimation of his normal sexual dynamism. Also, it does not match the official records' mention of a 'habitual crime'. The truth, then, would seem to lie somewhere between the two versions as remembered by Ridgeway's daughter and recounted by her son, Lord Tollemache, and the carefully rounded statements that lie in the Colonial Office papers.

Macdonald obviously did involve himself sexually with a number of schoolboys in Ceylon—Ridgeway later complained of a news-paper's attempts to "tamper with youths who gave evidence"—and his behaviour was sufficiently outrageous to cause a sensation in Ceylon's polite society, and to put pressure on the governor to rid the island of its prickly general. After years of sublimation, through hard service in Afghanistan, the Sudan and South Africa, it would appear that the psychological process that had channelled Macdonald's sex drive into safe, non-sexual areas, had broken down completely. But what the "habitual crime" was we have no way of telling. There is no mention of buggery, sodomy, indecency or conduct unbecoming an officer and gentleman; nothing of any legal substance exists in the Colonial Office papers and although a court martial was eventually ordered, there is no means of discovering the exact charges as the Judge-Advocate's records for Ceylon and India for the year 1903 are listed as 'missing' in the Public Record Office.

At worst, the "habitual crime" could only have been mutual masturbation with the schoolboys, a common enough offence which would not usually involve sexual assault. But it did take place in public, on a train, and thirty years earlier, as we have seen, misbehaviour with a young lady on a train had cost Valentine Baker his military career.

When Ridgeway decided to act he summoned Macdonald to his summer residence at Nuwara Eiya and made the suggestion that the only way out of the predicament was for Macdonald to return home immediately on an extended leave to consult with his superiors and to try to fix up an appointment elsewhere. From the reticence of the Ceylon press in the two months of February and March, it is logical to assume that Ridgeway had spoken to the editors of the leading newspapers (ironically, the editor of the *Ceylon Observer* was a Scot, and came from Easter Ross), and had asked them to maintain a veiled silence on the whole affair, as in all probablility, the general would not be returning to the island. In this, Ridgeway was acting in good faith as his telegram to the Colonial Office demonstrates. "Inform Secretary of State for War that General Macdonald leaves today on six months leave with my full approval. His immediate departure is essential to save grave public scandal which I cannot explain by telegraph. I take full responsibility for this unusual step, which my letter of today's mail to Lord Roberts justifies."[4] Ridgeway was entitled to grant a leave of absence to Macdonald and he gave it in the belief that his decision would be upheld by the next man to whom Macdonald would turn, the Chief of the Imperial General Staff, Lord Roberts of Kandahar.

Taking advantage of the presence of the London-bound liner, the S.S. *Ophir* in Colombo harbour, Macdonald set off for home on 19th February to determine his future course of action. The *Ophir* was an elegant, modern liner, built in 1901 for the round the world cruise made by the Duke and Duchess of York, and its route home took it via Port Said and Naples where other passengers were due to embark. Before leaving his headquarters at Slave Island, Macdonald made arrangements for the transfer of authority to his second in command, Lieutenant-Colonel J.C. Campbell of the Royal Engineers, and then granted a brief interview to the representative of the *Ceylon Observer:*

Asked as to the suddenness of his departure, Sir Hector preferred to offer no opinion, remarking, "Well, having got the telegram to return home at once, I took advantage of the *Ophir's* departure to leave immediately you see."

Sir Hector was reticent as to whether he was summoned to any special duty, and when our representative hazarded a guess as to Aden and Somaliland, he laughed it off with, "You want to know that, do you?" He expressed some curiosity as to how the information had got abroad, for he had only told a few of his friends before leaving Nuwara Eiya; but on second thoughts, Sir Hector evidently took a better view of local journalism, remarking that he supposed our reporter there knew he was coming away . . .

. . . The interview was terminated with, "Well, I am very sorry to go, you know; but I may come back again soon, eh?"[5]

Before leaving, Macdonald sent a carefully worded telegram to the governor as the liner slipped out of the Colombo roads. "Your Excellency's uniform kindness since I arrived in the Colony can never be effaced, and your manner of advising me now is proof of your continued kindness."

On board the *Ophir* were several Scots and they remarked upon the general's popularity and his good humour. A birthday party was arranged on 4th March and when the ship docked at Port Said he was befriended by a Gaelic-speaking minister, the Rev. Dr J.K. Campbell who later reported some of the misgivings entertained by the passengers from Ceylon. "When I parted from him at Naples, I said to him in Gaelic, 'Take care of yourself my friend. You have enemies as well as me or anybody, for jealousy is still as cruel as the grave.' I concluded by saying 'Blessings with you.' "[6] Apparently the rumours had followed him onto the ship and Campbell had heard the other passengers discussing Macdonald's lack of popularity in Ceylon.

When he arrived in London Macdonald booked into his club, the Army and Navy in Pall Mall and one of his first actions in the short time available to him was to go to Dulwich where his wife and son were living in conditions of relative middle-class comfort but also of total social obscurity. What transpired between them cannot be discerned but given Lady Macdonald's future actions it would appear to be most probable that he indicated to her the nature of the accusations and how he intended facing up to them. It was a sad ending to what had been a pitiful relationship and one that had brought little joy to either partner or to the son, Hector.

On Wednesday 18th March Macdonald had his first interview with Lord Roberts who had already been informed by Ridgeway of the exact nature of the case. The meetings continued the following day, too, behind the closed doors of the War Office and by Thursday evening Fighting Mac's fate had been fixed. Roberts told him categorically that he could not remain in the army unless he cleared his name. Although Roberts was known as a lenient man who disliked the idea of court martialling senior officers, he viewed Macdonald's case, for whatever reasons, as being so serious that the alternative of a posting elsewhere was not even considered. The rumour that King Edward VII was consulted does not have any basis in fact and it is most unlikely that he would have bothered himself with the matter, preferring instead to allow the process of the law to take its course. To that proposal, that he clear his name by court martial Macdonald reluctantly agreed and a reply was sent from the War Office to Ridgeway. "Under the circumstances the Commander-in-Chief does not propose to grant Sir Hector Macdonald the six months leave submitted by the Governor, as he does not desire to remove Macdonald from the ordinary process of the law."[7] There was now no way that the Governor in Ceylon could prevent questions from being asked in the Legislative Council nor to stop the press from reporting them.

The *Glasgow Herald* of 27th March presented a description of the events of the Thursday evening, all of which would have been witnessed by Roberts's personal staff. "This [the court martial] he begged to be allowed not to do, and a somewhat painful interview during which the late general burst into tears, resulted in his promising to go to France to think the matter over." And so on the following day, Friday 20th March, Macdonald set off again on the long haul back to Ceylon, his route taking him on the old P & O overland crossing from Dover, via Calais and Paris to Marseilles where the S.S. *Britannia* would take him first to Bombay. His fate had been sealed by Roberts who had written to Kitchener on the previous evening asking him to provide the necessary officers for a court martial in Ceylon. "Hector Macdonald goes back to Ceylon to be tried by a court martial. He sees his mistake in leaving his command without clearing his character, and I had to tell him that he could not remain in the Army, while such terrible accusations went unrefuted . . . he protests his innocence, but, if he is innocent, why on earth did he not insist upon having the matter cleared?"[8]

Macdonald arrived in Paris the same day and checked in at the Hotel Regina in the Rue du Rivoli, overlooking the Tuileries Gardens and near the Louvre. The hotel, a superb *fin de siecle* structure had been built at the beginning of the new century to cater for the fast-growing tourist trade and it was very popular with American and

British visitors. The general was obviously anxious to remain anonymous during those days of waiting: he was in mufti and the staff noted the sparsity of his baggage—only two simple suitcases and his valise. In the visitors book he signed himself 'H.A. Macdonald, London', and he took room 105, an unimposing bedroom on the first floor at the rear of the hotel. What he did over the weekend is impossible to piece together. Paris offered pleasures denied in London and he had been there before, *en route* to the Belgaum appointment in the previous year. "Never was Paris so crowded with the members of the English governing classes,"[9] wrote Frank Harris about the attraction of the French capital to British homosexuals during the eighteen-hundreds. Male brothels and pornography of all kinds flourished in the 'home of liberty' but it is a moot point whether or not Macdonald took advantage of what was on offer. The 'Great Beast' Aleister Crowley, caused a sensation by saying that he met Macdonald in the Hotel Regina where he called in to have lunch. "At the next table, also alone, was Sir Hector Macdonald. He recognised me and invited me to join him. He seemed unnaturally relieved: but his conversation showed that he was suffering acute mental distress. He told me that he was on his way to the East. Of course I avoided admitting that I knew his object, which was to defend himself against charges of sexual irregularity brought against him in Ceylon."[10] But if that was not sensational enough Crowley added an allegation that, after Macdonald's death, his trouser pockets were found to be crammed with pornographic pictures and that the story came to him from the British military attaché, Edward Montagu-Stuart-Wortley. It is an unlikely tale, as Montagu-Stuart-Wortley, an old friend of Fighting Mac, was not the man to spread gossip of that kind and if it had been true he would never have broadcast such a story.

In all probability, the later evidence that Macdonald kept himself to himself in Paris is true. He wrote a letter or two, went for solitary walks, took his lunch in the dining room where he met Aleister Crowley on Tuesday 24th March. It was on that day, too, that a letter arrived from the War Office informing him officially that he was to proceed to Ceylon to face a court martial. Also on that day in distant Ceylon Governor Ridgeway rose in the Legislative Council to answer a question about the whereabouts and future actions of the officer commanding the troops.

> It is known to all here that grave, very grave charges have been made against Sir Hector Macdonald. Although the offences charged are very serious, yet they are not punishable under Ceylon law, and, therefore,

cannot be the subject of an inquiry in a criminal court in this colony. When the charges transpired, General Macdonald, with my concurrence, and on my responsibility, went to England to consult his friends and superiors. He has desired to return to Ceylon and meet his charges, and I have been authorised to convene a court martial for this purpose. It is perhaps unnecessary for me to appeal to them [the press] to continue this honourable course, to remember that the case is practically *sub judice* and to say or suggest nothing prejudicial to the trial which every Englishman, every loyal subject, hopes will result, after a full and searching inquiry, in the complete and honourable acquittal of a soldier with so splendid a record of services to his King and country as General Macdonald.[11]

The die was now cast, as the press was free to report the proceedings of the Legislative Council and it did not take long for the Reuters correspondent to wing a report back to the newspapers of Britain and Europe. Macdonald's vain hope that the court would meet *in camera* was dashed. On the morning of 25th March, after a late breakfast, he walked into the small drawing-room off the foyer in which the daily newspapers were laid on a Louis Quatorze sidetable. He picked up a bundle and scanned the front pages, looking for the news that he dared to hope would never appear in print. His confusion was ended by the front page of the European edition of the *New York Herald*. There, beside a crude drawing of his features was the story that spelled his ruin. GRAVE CHARGE LIES ON SIR HECTOR MACDONALD: NOT AMENABLE TO LAW IN CEYLON HE SAILS FOR ENGLAND TO MEET THE CHARGE. What followed thereafter was, more or less, a verbatim report of Ridgeway's statement. Now the whole world would know.

Hotel staff were to say later that the general was stunned by what he had read. Carefully folding the newspapers, he put them under his arm and walked slowly up the curved staircase which took him to the first floor and the long, echoing corridor to room 105. Methodical to the last, he tidied his belongings and emptied his pockets on to the sidetable where also stood two unopened letters and the official signal from the War Office. He then removed his jacket and hung it in the wardrobe, and as a final gesture to the neatness that had characterised his life he took off his boots and put them under his bed. Then taking from his valise the small calibre eight millimetre gun he had probably bought the previous day, he checked the cylinder, and standing in front of the mirror he lifted the pistol to his right ear and pulled the trigger.

The bullet careered into his cranium, doing dreadful damage, and exited through the temple, taking with it most of the upper part of his brain. Death was instantaneous and the body crashed across the room, almost blocking the door where it lay, a growing pool of blood seeping darkly across the carpet. At two o'clock, two-and-a-half hours later, a maid tried to open the door of Macdonald's room, but finding her way blocked she called for the help of another member of staff, an assistant chef, and they found the dead general lying on the floor.

The manager, M. Tauber set in motion the machinery for the necessary legalities: the police were informed and Inspector Egartiler of the Palais Royal Quarter arrived to make a search of the room and expressed surprise at the general's meagre belongings, "no jewellery and very little money".[12] The French police report listed Macdonald as being dead by his own hand, and the British surgeon, Dr Gowring Middleton, who had been summoned by the British Consul General, certified Macdonald's death as "suicide from mental trouble". All that remained was the necessary official paperwork to remove the body later and to contact the general's relations about the funeral which would be held in Paris. Percy Inglis, the Consul General maintained a dignified silence over the whole matter and when questioned by an inquisitive French press about the nature of the suicide, he answered through Reuters that Macdonald was "a brave man, a very brave man".

In Ceylon the news was met with a sense of relief as no one had been looking forward to a trial which would have involved a senior British officer and the schoolboys from the train. Quite apart from the resultant harm that might have been done to the impressionable boys had they been forced to stand in the witness box to give evidence, most planters felt that such a case would weaken the authority of white rule in the colony and that the glorious sahibs would be seen to be as human as the next man. The consequences had been too awful for most of the white community to contemplate and a wave of sympathy went out to Sir West Ridgeway. Others, less prim perhaps, thought that the affair had been bungled and that Ridgeway's advice to Macdonald had been a mistake. It was felt in some quarters that even a local court martial held quickly behind closed doors could have cleared the case. If found guilty Macdonald could have retired early—it would have been an inglorious end to his career but at least his name would have been saved the recriminations and innuendoes that followed in the wake of the suicide.

On the following day, 26th March, the suicide was widely reported with expressions of sincere regret in the British and European press. Typical of the obituaries was the correctly restrained tone of the military correspondent of the *Westminster Gazette* in an article that

14

Not a Drum was Heard

According to local French law, the corpse of a suicide had to remain *in situ* for twenty-four hours before it could be removed, and so Macdonald's body lay overnight in a sealed-off room 105 after a short prayer had been said by the chaplain Mnr. Pedro Mesny. As a sign of respect, the hotel's manager cancelled the small orchestra which usually played each evening in the restuarant which looked out on to the Rue du Rivoli. The next day, embassy officials again arrived at the hotel and under police supervision the body was removed in a simple coffin to lie in state in the mortuary chamber of the British Embassy in the Rue d'Aguesseau. Suggestions, widely reported in the Scottish press, that the body was treated without respect, placed in a box and left in a broom cupboard, were stoutly denied by an indignant Consul General and confirmed by Pedro Mesny. If the Consul General and his staff erred it was in the premature announcement that Macdonald would be buried in Paris but that was probably because they were confused about the wildly differing messages from the War Office about Macdonald's next of kin.

In their records, the War Office listed William as the closest relation and there was no mention of a wife, but William was suffering from an attack of influenza and could not make immediate arrangements to respond to the War Office's telegram; it took a personal letter from the Aberdeenshire surgeon Dr Gowring Middleton who had attended on his brother's corpse to make him change his mind and to go to Paris to reclaim the body. He set off from Dingwall immediately, on the afternoon of Thursday 27th in the company of his cousin the Rev. James Macdonald who in popular acclaim to his more famous kinsman was known as 'Preaching Mac'. They reached Paris at 6.30p.m., having stopped *en route* at Perth to send a telegram to the Highland Society of London declaring that they placed themselves in the hands of the Scottish nation and that everything possible would be done to bring Hector back to Scotland. On arrival in Paris they went to the Consul General, determined to see their promise upheld, only to find it closed for the weekend. A caretaker directed them to the Rue d'Agusseau, but their luck was out. The body had left an hour ago in the company of another Mister Macdonald and would shortly be on its way to London.

Unbeknownst to the two upholders of the faith of the Scottish nation, young Hector and the family's Edinburgh solicitor Peter Morison, had contacted the War Office on the instructions of Lady Macdonald and had set off to Paris arriving two-and-a-half hours before the Dingwall delegation. They had immediately made arrangements for the body to be placed in a lead-lined and sealed coffin for return to Britain. It seems that Lady Macdonald, on hearing the news, had contacted the Adjutant-General, Sir Kelly Kenny, identified herself as next of kin and made rapid plans for a burial at dawn on Monday 30th March in Edinburgh. Satisfied that all was in order the Consul General's staff packed the coffin in a deal packing case, booked it on board the overnight Dieppe-Newhaven ferry and had it transferred to the Gare St Lazare. It was all very orderly and prevented further embarrassments. Besides, it was Saturday and the staff were anxious to get away, like other Parisians for 'le weekend'.

Accompanied by Dr Middleton, the Macdonalds, too, hurried to the station and were just in time to catch the same train and to confront young Hector and his solicitor. Both parties later made a good attempt at unity for the benefit of the press but it takes little in the way of deduction to guess that curt words were spoken, and the breach was to remain an open wound in the months to come. Thus William was denied the opportunity of viewing his brother's remains, however grisly a sight that might have been. There is no doubt that Lady Macdonald's intervention saved her husband's body from being buried in France but to the Dingwall Macdonalds and to the London Scots who were determined to honour the general, come what may, her actions were seen to be an insult not only to themselves but also in some grander, intangible way to what they felt to be the spirit of Scotland.

Their chance to reincarnate that spirit came on the evening of Sunday 29th at King's Cross railway station in north London. Macdonald's body had been taken to rest there after arriving in the city earlier that day, at 8 o'clock in the morning at London Bridge Station on the boat train from Newhaven. Total secrecy surrounded the arrival of the train and the porters carrying the heavy deal box had no idea what their load contained until a concerned station-master puffed along the platform to try to bring some solemnity to the proceedings. A plain parcels van backed into the platform and drove the box to King's Cross where it lay all day, identified only by its label 'H.A.M. Edinboro'.

An hour or so before the overnight train was due to leave at a quarter-to-nine the station began to fill up with a sombre crowd, some in Highland dress and all carrying flowers or wreathes. Amongst their number was Lady Jeune who tried in vain to make Lady Macdonald change her mind about the funeral arrangements, but she did succeed in persuading the station master to open the goods van's doors so that the huge crowd might place their tributes beside the coffin. She put her bunch of red roses on the coffin of a man who had been a special favourite of hers in the heady days after Omdurman, and behind her came a group of men representing the London Clans Society, the London Gaelic Society, the Ross, Sutherland and Cromarty Society and many other representatives of Scots in London including two members of parliamant, Sir William Allan and Galloway Weir. Also there was Dr Robertson, whose son had been a special correspondent of the general's and Miss Alice MacDonnell, bard to the Clan Macdonald Society.

The newspapers in London and Scotland went to great emotional lengths the following day to describe the "impressive scenes" as the van slowly filled with flowers while in the background a piper played Scotland's traditional air of lament, *The Flowers of the Forest*. Shortly after half-past-eight Lady Macdonald, her son Hector, and Peter Morison boarded the train and were followed by James and William who had been joined by his brother Ewan. Then the engine slowly gathered steam and the train drew out of the station on its four-hundred-mile journey north. Its departure was the signal for the majority of the crowd to troop into the neighbouring Great Northern Hotel where a public meeting was organised under the chairmanship of Galloway Weir MP. The gist of the meeting was that Lady Macdonald was wrong in ignoring the wishes of the Scottish people, but as the general's wife she was legally entitled to do as she thought fit, however much pressure had been brought to bear upon her.

After a good deal of wordy discussion which centered on Macdonald's heroic contribution to the Empire and the slight cast upon it by his widow, it was decided that the London Scots had done everything in their power to retrieve the situation and that it was now the turn of the home-based Scots. Telegrams were sent to the Lord Provosts of Edinburgh, Glasgow, Dundee and Aberdeen asking them to intercede on their behalf and messages were also sent to Edinburgh so that at least a token gathering would be available to welcome the overnight train. Few paid any attention to a Mr Mackenzie of the London Scottish Society who told the meeting that he had discussed the matter with Peter Morison and had learned that Lady Macdonald had taken the advice of the Lord Advocate, the crown prosecutor in Scotland, before proceeding with a quiet burial. As he sat in the compartment of the Edinburgh-bound train, Peter Morison, at least, must have known of the nature of the charges brought against his client's dead husband.

The first hint that all was not well with Macdonald had come in *The Scotsman* of 21st March. On the court page it was announced that the general would not be able to fulfill his promise of accepting the freedom of the City of Dundee "for some time as he would be leaving England at once", and "his health would not permit of his going north"—for it had become generally known that Fighting Mac had returned home on leave. Two days later the same page reported that King Edward VII had received Lieutenant-General Sir Kelly Kenny, the Adjutant-General in audience—no doubt to discuss Macdonald's impending court martial in Ceylon. It also carried a report of a dinner given by the Highland Societies of London to honour the Highland regiments, but although there were speeches galore and amongst those present were Roberts, Hamilton and Hunter, in contrast to earlier occasions, there is no mention of Macdonald. Even the weather in Scotland seemed to be in mourning, *The Scotsman* reporting high winds and heavy rain "roaring in the chimnies and the eerie moaning of overhead wires". For a nation nurtured on *Macbeth*, those were powerful portents.

When the news broke on Wednesday 25th March it sent shockwaves ringing through the country. "Sir Hector Macdonald (through Reuters' agency). Very grave charges are made against Sir Hector Macdonald the commander of the troops in Ceylon. When the charges were first brought, Sir Hector Macdonald, with the Governor's concurrence and His Excellency's responsibility went to England to consult his friends and his official superiors. He now returns to meet the charges, the Governor having been authorised to convene a court martial."[1] But on the following day the wave of surprise was halted in full flood by the horrid news that Hector was dead by his own hand in distant Paris. It was unbelievable. Not only was he dead but the first reports indicated that he was to be buried as a stranger in France and that Scotland was to be denied the opportunity of mourning her national hero. No one was yet to know of William's and James's frantic efforts, nor indeed of Peter Morison's and young Hector's movements between Paris and London. Lady Macdonald, for most people, did not exist. It was only after the meeting at the Great Northern Hotel had broken up and the night express had headed north that hurried telegrams could be sent to notable people in Edinburgh, including the Lord Provost James Steel asking them to intercede on the meeting's behalf for a stay of burial.

When the overnight train eased itself into Waverley Station at the early morning hour of five minutes to six, Peter Morison had seen to it that Lady Macdonald's funeral arrangements were to be carried out to the letter. A simple open-sided hearse and three funeral carriages had been arranged for the transport of the coffin and the family mourners to the Dean Cemetery which lies on an open plot of ground above the Water of Leith on the north-western approaches to the city. The service was to be taken by the Rev. Wallace Williamson and Dr Alexander Whyte of St George's United Free Church and they were on hand at Waverley to accompany the funeral procession. First, the coffin, now out of its packing case, was carried by the pall bearers to the waiting hearse, followed by the many wreaths and flowers that had been placed beside it at King's Cross. On the platform around one hundred people, mainly representatives of clan and Highland societies waited, their heads bare and bowed. Amongst their number was Hew Morrison, the city librarian, and a single officer in volunteer's uniform—on the strict instructions of Lady Macdonald not an officer was present from Scottish headquarters in Edinburgh Castle, although some newspapers did report one of their number in the crowd at the corner of Queensferry Street and Princes Street.

When the funeral cortège prepared to pull up the sloping entrance to the railway station there followed a somewhat undignified scramble amongst the crowd to reach their own cabs and carriages and the entire procession began its unstately way along Princes Street to the Dean Cemetery. "It must be rarely, indeed, that Edinburgh has known of a six o'clock funeral," wrote the novelist, Neil Munro, in the *Glasgow Evening News* of 31st March. "The Princes Street scavengers stared as the hearse trotted briskly past them, its dozen cabs behind; workmen walking on the bridge high over the village of Dean, looked and wondered, but they did not know that this was Hector Macdonald. How could they? He was being disposed of secretly—for so it was ordained—against the Will of all Scotland: the greatest precautions were taken to prevent the public from hearing where he was to go."

Other reports, too, spoke about the expressions of surprise seen in the faces of early morning workers as the procession made its way to the west end of Princes Street before turning north into Queensferry Street and over Telford's famous bridge to "the common-place suburban cemetery". His grave was a modest patch near the graveyard's northern wall and it gaped deep and open, ready to receive the coffin. Once the entire party was safely inside the grounds of the cemetery, the great iron gates were closed and Dr Whyte began his simple ceremony, opening with the 130th Psalm, "Out of the depths have I cried unto thee, O Lord" and taking his text from Revelations VI. There followed a short benediction and the coffin was lowered gently into the grave with the saddest of all sounds, the earth breaking on its oaken lid. The whole service was reminiscent in form and content of the funeral given to Macdonald's fellow countryman, Hugh Miller, who committed suicide in Edinburgh in 1856 and who lies buried in the Grange Cemetery.

William and his new-found sister-in-law were visibly shaken by the proceedings which lasted little more than twenty minutes and at its conclusion each would go their separate ways—William and James left for Dingwall on the 10.15a.m. train to decide what, if anything, could be done to retrieve a situation that had been lost so dramatically in Paris on the previous Saturday. Exhausted by three days' hard travelling, they returned north to campaign again for the retrieval of what they saw as the family's lost honour. Lady Macdonald and Hector remained in Edinburgh with Peter Morison, all probably aware that they would have to bear the brunt of the allegations that would be thrown against them by an angry nation once it was discovered that the War Office was not responsible for the funeral arrangements. The northern Scottish towns which had so honoured him after Omdurman were the most affected by the news of the sudden burial in Edinburgh and it was suggested that as it was a matter of national pride, family obligations should have been put to one side. An acrimonious correspondence developed between Lady Macdonald and the people of Dingwall. In reply to the town council's motion of regret, she wrote to the town clerk a studied letter dated 4th April, explaining her reasons. "My son and I then fixed that my husband should rest in Edinburgh. To this we were moved by reasons personal to ourselves, reasons which I explained to those who called to press the claims of persons in other localities. Further, I wished the funeral to be private, not merely because it was my own desire, but mainly because I know that my husband would have wished it to be so." In other words, she was only exercising the widow's prerogative but those hostile to her would not have been mollified by her closing words. "Unfortunately, some people who misunderstood my feelings attempted to alter my plans. I readily forgive them, because I know it was from love of my husband that their mistaken actions sprang."

Amongst those "people who misunderstood" was cousin James and his response was a furious letter of 24th April, made available to the press, which referred to his confusion when "we were surprised to find that the matter had passed out of our hands by the appearance of a widow whose son and agent were despatched to Paris to claim the body and effects". So angry was the letter and so indelicate its phrasing that *The Scotsman* was moved to defend Lady Macdonald a day later. "A widow and a son are infinitely nearer to a dead husband and father than any cousin and the Rev. Mr Macdonald's way of referring to a lady, who throughout one of the most trying ordeals which a member of her sex could undergo, has conducted herself with rare judgement and prudence, is deplorably lacking in that charity which one naturally expects from a member of his cloth."

But as more details were released, the more annoyed the Macdonalds became with their kinswoman. The War Office, through Sir Kelly Kenny, had offered the use of a gun carriage to convey the coffin across London and a military funeral could have been arranged in Edinburgh. General Sir Archibald Hunter, Macdonald's comrade from Sudan days, and then in Edinburgh commanding the Scottish Division, had asked to be present at the funeral. Pressure was put on Lady Macdonald when she arrived in Edinburgh to at least allow the funeral to take place at a decent hour of day. To all those suggestions she turned a deaf ear and for her pains she was to become the target of much antagonism. Her reasons for wanting privacy lay perhaps in the visit Sir Hector had made to her in Dulwich before setting off again for Ceylon. If he had told her the nature of the charges that were to be brought against him, it is understandable that Lady Macdonald must have hoped that a quiet funeral would bury the whole matter without any untoward fuss. She was also a retiring and modest person who disliked being in the limelight which had been thrust upon her so suddenly—her title, in effect, only came into being with the death of her husband as no one had known of her prior existence.

Nevertheless, as the legal representative of the general she had to defend her stand and in addition to writing letters of explanation she was forced to take legal action against ex-Councillor Wallace Thom of Glasgow when a privately printed pamphlet, dated April 1903, entitled *The Idol of the Scottish Nation* called her a "revengeful woman". It continued, "that intolerable spite of the woman will mature the warrior plant dumped into Dean Cemetery ground the other morning: till from it will rise a forest of lasting monuments, thicker than the Caledonian forests of old, in every colony and protectorate of the King's domains".[2] In another part of the diatribe Thom also suggested that Macdonald's crime was "loving his Governor's daughter". (There is a lot of misunderstanding about Ridgeway's children. His only daughter, Violet Aline, married Brigadier E.D.H. Tollemache in 1909 and their son is the present Lord Tollemache.) Lady Macdonald sued Thom and won her case before Lord Stormonth-Darling, ironically, the same judge who had regularised her marriage in 1894.

At the end of an emotional day, Monday 30th March, the first visitors came to the Dean Cemetery. Amongst them was Lady Macdonald who left a wreath of lilies in the shape of a heart, but there were many strangers, too, as the word went around the city that Hector had been buried in Edinburgh. A steady trickle of visitors continued throughout the week but they were nothing compared to the scenes that materialised on the following weekend. A large crowd queued patiently on the Saturday to pay its last respects, but on the Sunday, it being a brilliantly sunny Spring day, the crowds were even more spectacular. By mid-morning, at least 30,000 people waited outside the gates of the cemetery to pay homage to a hero whom everyone there looked on as being second only in importance to William Wallace and Robert the Bruce.

> From every district of the city they traced their steps towards the Dean Cemetery. The directors of the Cemetery Company had resolved to keep the gates shut until twelve o'clock, and long before mid-day, a crowd of several thousands stood around the east or main entrance waiting admission. Under the supervision of Inspector Moyes a staff of 40 constables was on duty, and in order to prevent the occurrence of any unseemly incident or unnecessary jostling, they immediately proceeded to form a queue. As the afternoon wore on immense crowds thronged all the thoroughfares leading to the eastern gate, which was the only one opened. A goodly number arrived in carriages and cabs, but the great majority were on foot, and at half-past three the crowds in the cemetery were so dense that one might have imagined some great football match was about to take place.[3]

Hardly a day passed during the week of 6th April but that *The Scotsman* did not also report equally enthusiastic crowds anxious to leave some token of respect by the graveside. A large delegation of mourners arrived from Dingwall and followed the funeral route to the cemetery where a short service of dedication was held, and wreaths poured in from all over the world. A large box containing two laurel wreaths was sent to Dingwall from Macdonald's admirers in Paris, one of whom was thought to be the "anonymous American financier" who was to fund the unofficial commission of enquiry. Its card read simply: "Laurels to the Great Dead from strangers which are denied to him where he earned them". But it was in Edinburgh that the greatest floral tributes were to be paid and wreaths continued to be left by anonymous individuals and also by representatives of institutions representing every level of Scottish life. There were flowers and wreaths from Australia and New Zealand and it was reported that Edinburgh florists had to work overtime in the fortnight after the funeral. Gradually the crowds melted away and Macdonald became another tragedy for Scotland to brood upon. A modest memorial stone and bronze bust were later erected on the site of the grave which is still a landmark in the cemetery to this day.

Militarism in Scotland had, perhaps, reached its zenith during the Edwardian period and the events of the Boer War had excited much popular protest and anti-Boer feeling. "On Mafeking Night, traffic in Glasgow was brought to a standstill by a procession of shipyard workers with flags and banners, and an effigy of President Kruger labelled To St Helena."[4] All over Scotland there were celebrations as hearty as any seen south of Hadrian's Wall and an air of great mutual self-congratulation was felt throughout the country because it was a Scotsman's, Sir Archibald Hunter's Tenth Divsion that had raised the siege. Magersfontein, as we have seen, had been met with incredulity, but it was being amply avenged by many good Scots in positions of power and Fighting Mac's Highland Brigade had been busy recovering its lost pride.

Newspapers were full of the war and manufacturers had used its images, including the faces of the generals, to promote sales. Jingoism was not a dirty word and going off for a soldier had become a noble duty. Very few heeded the words of a handful of radicals who had seen in the Boer War the shape of things to come and the mass slaughter, thirteen years later, of a volunteer army "doing its duty". We may smile today, or shake our heads at the mass adulation given to Hector Macdonald and at the almost spiritual surprise which met the news of his death in Scotland, but set against the spirit of the age and the prevailing climate of political opinion, he was seen, rightly, as a hero and a popular idol, in the same style as today's heroes, football stars and popular singers.

15

Von Mackensen and other Myths

Within days of the announcement of Macdonald's death and the news of the untimely burial, the rumours began. Highland and clan societies—especially those of the Macdonalds and the Mackays, two of the great Ross and Cromarty families—convened hastily arranged meetings to discuss what might be done to honour the general's name. There were many who felt a keen personal sense of insult at the stealthy way in which their hero had been buried in Edinburgh and they were quick to voice their disapproval. The Clan Macdonald Society of London was the first to promote the idea of a memorial and this was taken up enthusiastically by William and his cousin James who were still smarting at the way in which Lady Macdonald had appeared from the wings to claim Hector's body. Not to be outfaced, the town council of Dingwall placed it on record that their royal burgh was the proper place for the siting of a monument to the "burgess general", and the minutes of that meeting, held on 1st April, also record the sense of "outrage", not only to "the feelings of the Highlands, but also to the feelings of every British person and every Colonial who owned Britain as his home". Discussion in Dingwall, and in the many clan societies from all over the world who made contributions, centred on raising enough money to commemorate a man whom many Scots felt to be innocent of any crimes that he was said to have committed in faraway Ceylon. There were calls, too, for the re-opening of the case, linked to a strongly-voiced feeling that Macdonald's file had been closed with indecent haste and that the true facts would never be known.

A heated correspondence developed in Scotland's two national newspapers, *The Scotsman* and *The Glasgow Herald*, with writers pointing out that had Macdonald been a member of a higher social caste his friends would have leaped to his defence instead of allowing him to journey back to Ceylon alone to face a set of unsubstantiated charges. Those were matched by a handful of letters begging for dignified silence lest Macdonald's reputation be ruined by unfortunate discoveries. Let him rest in peace was the general feeling. But those mediators were dismissed angrily by more vehement correspondents who felt that Scotland had been insulted in public by what they chose to see as the government's tardy treatment of one of her favourite sons. Typical of those was a letter to *The Glasgow Herald* on 2nd April, written by one 'J.McI' who thundered his disapproval in a powerful rhetoric.

> It is the most cowardly, unheroic display of do-nothingness that history has yet recorded. And these are the men we send to win our battles. Some of them are dubbed Field Marshals and Generals and even possess that coveted symbol of valour the Victoria Cross, but alas they are not soldiers, only officers; that's why our battles are lost. God pity them, Scotsmen do.

Others joined in and when an anonymous American financier (it may have been Andrew Carnegie) was said to have offered £10,000 for a fund to clear Macdonald's name, there were calls for a giant meeting in the St Andrews Halls in Glasgow with the threefold aims of discovering the truth of the charges brought against Macdonald, clearing his name, and bringing about the downfall of those held to have been responsible for besmirching it.

Although an unofficial 'commission' was eventually formed and travelled to Ceylon to gather evidence, nothing came of the moves to hold mass protest meetings in Glasgow or in any other town. Gradually the letter writers turned their attention to other matters such as Irish Home Rule and Michael Davitt's proposed visit to Glasgow later that year, and to the impending Royal visit to Scotland. But in the midst of all the indignation and pent-up rage that characterised the Macdonald correspondence one sensible letter stands out. It was written in *The Glasgow Herald* which had taken the most positive interest in the affair ("the public will not rest until it knows why the remains of Sir Hector Macdonald have not been accorded that moderate respect that would have been accorded in a decorous funeral in Edinburgh at the ordinary hour or in a quiet funeral in his own country," ran the editorial of 31st March). Because it makes such a pertinent, though never resolved point, that anonymous letter of 3rd April is worth quoting in full.

> In the Army List there are some instructive pages devoted to the 'special lists' of which one is a special list of "officers receiving awards for distinguished and meritorious services'. Put as shortly as possible, these are:

	Cav/Inf	Art/Eng	Indian	Total
Field Marshal	1	—	—	1
Generals	7	8	—	15
Lt Generals	16	12	4	31
Maj Generals	41	11	13	65
Colonels	24	7	7	38
	89	38	24	150

In addition to the above there are about 100 officers of lower rank in the home and Indian army enjoying rewards. What these rewards are I am not in a position to say but no doubt they are pecuniary and in the case of the higher ranks are probably substantial. Why does one look in vain in this list for the name of Macdonald? We are content to remain unenlightened as to some of the closing incidents in his career, but I think we are entitled to know why a soldier conspicuous if ever man was for 'distinguished and meritorious service' did not receive the reward given to other men whom I need not name. I commend the list to the careful perusal of those to whom an Army List is accessible.

It was true. Macdonald had not received one penny of bounty for his part in the South African War, although he had, of course received rewards of another kind in his knighthood and in the appointment of paid A.D.C. to King Edward VII. Why had Macdonald been excluded from the "distinguished and meritorious" service list? Sixty-five officers of the rank of major-general received cash awards, many of whom would not have had such a distinguished command as that of the Highland Brigade. One reason lay in Macdonald's own reticence. He had been convinced that public exposure in the press would harm his career and when well meaning friends wanted to mount a campaign to promote his case, he begged them to desist their efforts. The letter was never followed up and the reasons for the granting of cash awards to some but not to others lie buried in the inscrutable fastness of the criteria for public patronage and honours.

The very secrecy and the deepening silence in official circles only served to prolong the controversy. It was natural enough for there to have been a public outcry over Lady Macdonald's bizarre funeral arrangements and over the hazy mention of unspecified charges, but these were to be but little compared to the flurry of wild rumours that began to circulate in Scotland. A man calling himself John Barron telegrammed the *Dundee Courier and Advertiser* with a weird message: "Tell Scotland that powerful friends will soon prove General Hector Macdonald guiltless of every iniquity charged against him. Blackmail, malice and official jealousy saddled him with circumstantial evidence which he was too poor to fight and the ingratitude of supposed friends did the rest. To give further details of them would defeat justice." In Glasgow, D.P. Menzies, a prominent businessman, addressed the Clan Macdonald Society with some stunning, though far-fetched evidence, which was reported in *The Scotsman* of 1st April: "He thought it just possible that the death of Sir Hector Macdonald might not have been caused by suicide. It might have been accidental and there were also circumstances which pointed to a possibility of assassination. Macdonald had evidently been shadowed by an individual in Paris and if the body were thoroughly investigated it might be found that the wound was not caused by a revolver shot but by a stilletto. No key was found in the door."

Where his information came from, it is now impossible to discover. Macdonald did not meet people in Paris, if contemporary press reports are correct, but the bullet wound behind the right ear with the exit in the temple *is* inconsistent with a suicide attempt, although there is nothing to suggest that it is impossible. The post mortem showed conclusively that Macdonald had died in Paris and the death certificate spelled out his fate: *'Macdonald, suicide par arme a feu'*. Most suicide attempts in the head though, are made with a bullet fired into the side of the head, through the mouth or into the temple, and there were many who believed that the method of Macdonald's dispatch was more in keeping with an execution, with the victim lying spread-eagled on the floor and being shot in the rear of the head. Newspaper reports stated that in his hand was a small calibre pistol which would have made his self-destruction an easy task, but sceptics wanted to believe that he would have used his heavy Mark IV Webley (introduced in 1889 and widely used during the Boer War) which is so powerful that it would have blown most of his head away if used at such a close range. But the chances were that Macdonald would not have been carrying his own hand gun. At some point during his four days in Paris he could have purchased an 8-millimetre pistol of the kind that were then so popular in both France and America as a means of self-defence.

Then there was the matter of the corpse. William Macdonald was denied the opportunity of viewing his brother's remains and he went to his own grave in 1930 lamenting his failure to press home his rights. As we have seen, the body was kept in custody in a lead-lined coffin before making its hurried journey back to Edinburgh to an early morning funeral, and that secret haste was to fan the rumour that Fighting Mac had been done away with and that his coffin contained only a pile of stones. It was a theory that many wanted to believe but it does not take into account the fact that Macdonald was certified dead by the British surgeon in Paris and, more importantly, his remains were also identified by his old friend from Sudan days, Lieutenant-Colonel Edward Montagu-Stuart-Wortley. He had been one of the first to arrive at the Hotel Regina, in his capacity as military attaché, and he had been very upset to discover the suicide in room 105. The following day he broke all the diplomatic rules by writing to the editor of the Paris edition of the *New York Herald* complaining about the reporting of a matter that had not yet reached the stage of jurisdiction. At the end of a dignified letter he put his feelings directly and forcibly about the "worst possible taste" shown in the front-page report. "The loss to the British army of one of its most distinguished officers, under circumstances which were most distressing, is sufficiently great; but you have considerably added to the pain of it by your manner of announcing it."

Strangest of all, when Macdonald's son's ashes were interred in the family grave in 1951, the gravediggers reported that they could not reach the general's coffin because it was covered with a mixture of mortar and stones. Without re-interring the remains today, that story, which was kept alive for many years by the workers in the cemetery, is impossible to prove or disprove. The rubble could owe its existence to a rumoured attempt to dig up the remains shortly after the burial so that Macdonald could sleep in his own country amongst his own countrymen. Certainly, a police watch had to be kept at the Dean Cemetery for several days after the funeral.

The theory that he had been murdered continued to linger on in many people's minds and around it was created a new rumour. Macdonald was not dead at all. The body was that of someone else: a suicide had been faked and Macdonald had changed his identity. Like King Arthur he was waiting in hiding for the hour when his country would need him most. One story had it that he was holed up in an Edinburgh house under secret guard and that rumour was fueled when an unknown man jumped to his death from the South Bridge into the Cowgate a few years later. Witnesses said that he was the spitting image of Fighting Mac.

Others said that he had abandoned Britain for another country. Brigadier Cannot, a friend of Sir Ian Hamilton's was convinced that he had seen Macdonald in the uniform of a Japanese officer during the Russo-Japanese War and that "the recognition was immediately mutual, that both of them refrained from speech, that during the time he was with the Japanese army he saw Macdonald four or five times."[1] And there were many more unsubstantiated reports from other parts of the world. A Skyeman confirmed the story of the Japanese connection, saying that his father, a merchant seaman, had seen Macdonald in Japanese soldier's uniform at a military review in

Tokyo in 1910 and probably because Japan seemed remote and exotic that story gained a powerful currency.[2] Another popular theory had it that he had assumed the identity of the Russian General Kuropatkin and when Macdonald's son Hector, by then an engineer, visited Russia in 1911 on a business trip, it was thought by those who believed the myths that he was merely paying his father a visit. It is an unlikely theory. Young Hector had left Dulwich College in 1905 and had then trained as an engineer. Most of his life was spent in North Shields and from the most tangible account of his circumstances he became "warped, a bitter man, latterly a recluse",[3] one who wanted to have nothing to do with his father's memory. A friend of Lady Macdonald's, Dr James Muirhead, described him as "a prickly customer, dour and taciturn"[4] who remembered his father on the few occasions that he saw him, as a strict, authoritarian man. Before his death, young Macdonald gave some of his father's belongings to Dingwall Town Council and the medals were presented to the Scottish United Services Museum in Edinburgh Castle, but on the whole, he had affected to despise his father's memory and he was not close enough to him to have made a special visit to see him in 1911.

When a great man dies, it's a common enough phenomenon for his friends and admirers to disbelieve mortality and to cling to the vain hope that the grave has been cheated. History is littered with reports of sightings of well-known men after their supposed deaths and the more mysterious the manner of their departure, the stronger the faith in the story. Napoleon, Czar Nicolas II, Commander Crabbe, Hitler and Glen Miller are only a few, very different, examples of men who are supposed to have survived their "official" deaths and to have lived on under different identities elsewhere. So it was thought too that Fighting Mac was still alive somewhere on the globe, and friends, startled by the rumours, remembered his interest in studying languages and that shortly before his death he had been mastering German and was deeply caught up in studying their military tactics (Macdonald's views on conscription were thought by many to be too "teutonic"). Had he gone across to the Germans? That story was nurtured and kept alive even during the First World War when a new set of military heroes made ready to march out on to the world's stage and, lemming-like, to sacrifice themselves and others in the holocausts of France and Belgium. The Highland regiments, like other line regiments of the British imperial armies, did their bit on the Western Front. Amongst their numbers, in the early days of the war at least, were seasoned campaigners of the Boer War and they chose not to forget Macdonald. They liked the notion that Fighting Mac had gone across to the Hun and told it amongst themselves that he would never order his troops against them. For that reason he was away in the east somewhere, fighting in a little known place that the politicians called the Balkans. His name? Field-Marshal August von Mackensen, the Death's Head Hussar.

The story went like this. For some years the Germans had known of Macdonald's homosexual tendencies and had set about blackmailing him. In return for military information they shielded his secret from the British authorities but by 1903 the position was becoming intolerable and Macdonald asked to be lifted. A suicide was rigged in the Hotel Regina, Macdonald went across to the Germans and took the place of von Mackensen, an officer who was conveniently dying of cancer in a Breslau clinic. Yes, by God, Hector had got the better of Kitchener and his like in the end! The story was resurrected in the summer of 1962 when an ex-Foreign Office official, G.A. Minto, writing in the June issue of *Blackwood's Magazine* claimed to have seen a German document which was dropped on the British lines during the First World War. It tells the same story with a good deal of bravado and hinted, none too subtly that Macdonald was now a German officer:

> Is it not marvellous that one of our most famous commanders was born a Scottish peasant? Field Marshal von Mackensen, conqueror of the Balkans, began life as a common soldier in the British army. He fell into disgrace and entered the service of the Kaiser in the name of another officer who was on the point of death.[5]

The story—as I first read it *en route* from Harwich—was taken up by Edgar Lustgarten in the *Sunday Express* and the controversy broke out yet again. Both writers made much of the propaganda document (which has never been traced and must therefore be discounted as hard evidence) and of the the secrecy that surrounded Macdonald's movements in Paris. The shadowy facts of von Mackensen's early life were also commented upon, and Lustgarten in particular, pointed to the absense of complete military records for both men. The leaflet theory is an attractive one but even if the document could be found there is a good case, too, for writing it off as a crude piece of propaganda, the Germans capitalising on the rumours that were rife in British society. Minto himself points to the clever use made of propaganda by Bismarck—and by later politicians—who leaked embarrassing news to the press when a political opponent had to be discredited. Many of those appeared under the pseudonym of Baron von Holstein—could the von Mackensen/Macdonald story belong to that *genre*?

There was a strongly held belief in Britain during the First World War that the Germans possessed a *cabinet noir* of British homosexuals in prominent public positions and that the information about their private lives was used to blackmail them in return for official secrets. The person who was supposed to have supplied them with most of the original information was Mrs George Keppel who had at one time been the mistress of the Prince of Wales. In 1918 the story was taken up by Noel Pemberton Billing, a notoriously anti-homosexual MP who claimed in his right-wing journal *Imperialist* (later and more sinisterly known as *The Vigilante*) that an anonymous British officer had shown him evidence of the 1,000-page book in which the sexual peculiarities of people in high places were listed in extraordinary detail. Again, there is no evidence that such a book existed, although it did become the principal subject of a libel action involving Billing and an actress, Maud Allan, in which one of Billing's defence witnesses claimed that she had been shown a copy of the book by Neil Primrose MP, the son of the Earl of Rosebery.[6] The case had been brought by Maud Allan who accused Billing of libelling her as a lesbian in his journal, but such was the anti-homosexual fervour aflame in Britain that Billing was acquitted and declared a hero of public morality. The black book may have had a shadowy life of its own and why should not the Germans, or the British, have taken an interest in the sexual tastes of their enemy's leading men and women? The twentieth century has seen a number of espionage cases related to sex and blackmail and the homosexual recruiting of spies amongst Cambridge undergraduates became a public scandal from the nineteen-fifties onwards with the defection of Burgess and Maclean and the downfall of Antony Blunt. Macdonald's homosexuality could have been a security risk but would it have been possible for him to have assumed another man's identity as the leaflet is supposed to have alleged?

August von Mackensen was one of the most distinguished officers in the army of Kaiser Wilhelm II. A handsome, elegant man who claimed in his old age to have kept the figure of a subaltern, he wore the startling black uniform of the Death's Head Hussars with its busby crowned by a white skull. He had been born on 6th December 1849 and after being privately tutored he was educated at the University of Halle before becoming an officer cadet at the age of nineteen. He fought in the Franco-Prussian War and thereafter his rise through the officered ranks was steady, if unspectacular. He had accompanied the Kaiser on his tour of Palestine in 1898 and in his role as adjutant he acquired a dashing reputation for his spectacular six-foot black-booted figure and for the courtliness of his behaviour in public. In 1903 he was a major-general commanding the 36th Division in Danzig, that same year he was promoted lieutenant-general on the 11th September and five years later he was a full general in command of the 17th Army Corps. At the outbreak of the First World War his dashing cavalry operations against the Russians on the eastern front earned him promotion to field-marshal in 1915 and the rest of his war was spent in Serbia and Rumania. Thereafter his life was full of public honour and even though he retired from the army in 1920 his hussar-uniformed figure was a well-known sight at public occasions.

In 1879 he had married Dorothea von Horn and by that marriage he had two daughters and three sons between 1883 and 1897. His wife died in December 1905 and he married again, Leonie von der Osten on 29 April 1908, the year of his promotion to general. If a transfer had been made Macdonald would have had to adopt an ailing wife for the better part of two years and would also have taken on four children (one daughter had died), the youngest a watchful six-year old daughter called Ruth. There was also the matter of von Mackensen's mother, a sternly patriotic lady who was not to die until May 1916 and who had taken no little interest in her son's affairs. Elsewhere, an entire army division and the whole of the German general staff would have had to keep this terrible and improbable secret.

During the Nazi period von Mackensen was to be a focus for many disaffected officers from the old army; one of his sons was to serve as a general in Italy and he himself was to remain faithful unto death to his king and emperor. When Wilhelm II died in Holland in 1941 the elderly field-marshal was the only survivor from a bygone age to pay the last respects to his sovereign. As the grave was made ready and the last respects made, von Mackensen, with tears in his eyes, offered his own private gesture to the man to whose loyalty he owed his own success: he carefully laid his cavalry cloak over the coffin and saluted the shades of old Prussia. His own days were also numbered and he died on 8th March 1945 in Celle near Hanover at the venerable age of ninety-six. There is no doubt that the man in the Death's Head Hussar uniform who fascinated the British officers who visited him was August von Mackensen and not Sir Hector Macdonald. Amongst the men who called at his home was a party of Royal Scots Greys under Major Tim Lewis who, despite the British policy of non-fraternisation, still saluted the old officer as one cavalryman to another. Later they were to remark on the field-marshal's erect, soldierly bearing—even in old age he was still a good four inches taller than Macdonald had ever been.[7]

Two inconsistencies, though,—those subtle wings of rumour and deceit that help to fan any controversy—commend themselves for attention. In his official writings, von Mackensen spent much energy stoutly denying that his name had any Scottish origins. It came from the village of Maccenhausen in Westfalia he argued in an autobiographical note in 1938. *'Die in Schottland verbreitete und gelegentlich auch in Deutschland lautgewordene Ansicht meine Familie stamme aus Schottland ist Legende. Das Geschlecht der Mackensen ist rein deutschen Ursprungs. Nach einer Staatsarchiv zu Münster Westfalen ruhenden Urkunde sassen sie bereits in Jahre 1144 am Ostfuss der Solling im heutigen Mackenussen, damals Maccenhussen und Maccenhausen geschrieben als Lehnsleute und Ministeriaten der bei der Stadtoldendorf sitzenden grafen von Homburg und nannten sich wie der Ort.'*8* It was not derived from Mackenzie—but it could have been. During the seventeenth and eighteenth centuries many Scots made a habit of visiting the Baltic countries as merchants or as mercenaries in exile and if, for example, Learmonth could have become Lermontov in Russia, could not the same be said, as was said in some quarters in Scotland, that the names of Mackenzie and Mackensen were one and the same? Even a recent military *Companion* states that "before 1914 Mackensen boasted of his Scottish descent".9 It was obvious enough that during the First World War, the field-marshal would have wanted to hide any trace of British connections, but even though his position would have been honoured and secure in the nineteen-thirties it would have done little harm for his antecedents to be 'rein deutsch' in the days of Hitlerian racial purity. And in any case, von Mackensen was a proud old patriot who loved his fatherland: in his old age the thought that his name could have been of Scottish origin would have been anathema to him.

The second quirk in von Mackensen's personality was his habit of kissing the Kaiser's hand. Up until 1904, when he introduced it at court, polite bowing was considered the extent to which familiarity could be carried towards the Royal family. Most army officers were Prussians and the practice was considered distasteful, being looked on as unmilitary, or at worst, unmanly. It was a practice considered

*The point of view, widely expressed in Scotland and now in Germany, that my family originates in Scotland, is a myth. The Mackensen family's origins are pure German. According to an extant document in Múnster Westfalen, by the year 1144, they were tenants on the east bank of the Solling in the Mackenussen of today, but then called Maccenhussen or Maccenhausen, where they were burgesses of the town of Oldendorf, a seat of the Counts of Homburg; and they called themselves after the name of the place.

16

Aftermath

After a good deal of discussion between the London Scots and Dingwall Town Council over the siting of a memorial to Sir Hector, it was eventually agreed to accept the suggestion of the Glasgow joint clan societies that Dingwall, the capital of Ross and Cromarty, Macdonald's home county, should house the monument when it was built. Money for its erection poured into the fund established in Macdonald's name and the foundation stone was laid on the Mitchell Hill overlooking the town on 25th September 1905. It was laid in a simple ceremony by D.H. Macdonald, chairman of the Glasgow Committee, who was thanked by Galloway Weir, MP. The hollow, square, castellated structure with its inner staircase was built, unusually, from the inside outwards, without the aid of scaffolding and its present, broken-tooth facade still dominates the skyline in the cemetery above the town. It was opened officially on Thursday 23rd May 1907 at a ceremony attended by several thousand well-wishers, many of whom had been present at the granting of the freedom of the town to Macdonald eight happier years earlier. Lady Macdonald and her son were also present: it was to be their final connection with the countrymen of Macdonald's birth. Lady Macdonald died four years later and lies buried in her husband's grave in Edinburgh after living in quiet obscurity in Newcastle.

At the road-end where the track from Rootfield meets the main road, the people of Mulbuie erected their own unpretentious monument to their famous son. It stands near the schoolhouse where Alexander Treasurer gave him his early education, and on a clear day, if you look westwards, the dark outline of the Dingwall monument can be seen on the Mitchell Hill, some four or five miles away. Other moves were set afoot to honour his name but they came to naught, every effort being put into the subscriptions for the monuments. Amongst the better of the suggestions came from a pressure group who wanted to see the Queen Victoria School at Dunblane, which provides a boarding school education for the children of army personnel, named for Macdonald but the claims of the former sovereign were obviously going to outweigh those of a major-general's, however famous he may have been. The press took an interest in the affair for a month or two after the suicide by publishing letters and items about the memorial fund, but his name soon disappeared from their columns: he simply was not news any more. In its place came a score of poems, ranging from the passable to the execrable, most of which contented themselves with the sentiment that whatever his faults—and we don't want to know those!—Hector was a brave son of the soil who should be allowed to rest in peace. Best amongst them is Robert Service's poem sub-titled *A Life Tragedy* whose opening lines get nearer the truth than perhaps the poet himself realised.

> A pistol-shot rings round and round the world:
>   In pitiful defeat a warrior lies.
> A last defiance to dark Death is hurled,
>   A last wild challenge shocks the sunlit skies.
>   Alone he falls with wide, wan, woeful eyes:
> Eyes that could smile at death—could not face shame[1]

More importantly, in the aftermath of his death, questions were asked in the House of Commons about the manner of the announcement of the charges by West Ridgeway. Major F.C. Rasch, the M.P. for Chelmsford addressed a question to the Secretary of State for India asking why Ridgeway had made public the news about the impending court martial. It was answered, properly, by Joseph Chamberlain, the Secretary of State for the Colonies who retorted that the Governor's remarks had been reported in the British press from his statements to the Legislative Council in Ceylon, as Ridgeway was duty-bound to do. "No such dispatch has been published, and I think the Hon. and Gallant Gentleman must be referring to a report which I myself saw in *The Times* of an answer given by Sir West Ridgeway to a question addressed to him by an independent member of the Ceylon Legislative Council. The proceedings of the Legislative Council are published, and it is open to anyone to telegram such an answer, but no dispatch of the sort has been received."[2] Pressed further by Rasch to agree that it was wrong to condemn a man before he had been heard, Chamberlain replied that Macdonald had not been condemned by anyone in any statement and that everybody, he was sure, hoped that the charges would have been disproved. The case was taken up by Galloway Weir, the MP for Macdonald's county but the government stuck to the official line that the court martial was a matter for Ceylon and that the letter of the law had been adhered to most faithfully.

But the Macdonalds and many other Scots continued to believe that Fighting Mac had been framed, that the charges were without substance and that he was the victim of jealousy and hatred amongst the upper echelons of Ceylon society or in the army's high command. Shortly after the suicide, an anonymous American financier, popularly though to have been Andrew Carnegie, offered £10,000 for the establishment of a commission to prove Macdonald innocent and to declare that there was "evidence to prove beyond a shadow of a doubt that the allegations against the character and conduct of the dead general are nothing but reports circulated by jealous and interested persons who have never forgiven him for rising from the ranks".[3] There is nothing in the way of firm evidence about the funding of this so-called 'Committee of Scots' and it is impossible to prove whether or not the benefactor was Andrew Carnegie. By 1903 he had made his major awards to the British library and education systems and was retired from business. But through his interest in the north of Scotland—he had bought Skibo Castle in Sutherland in 1898—and his concern for the underdog and the hero, he could well have been in a position to have provided funds for a commission to prove Macdonald innocent. The fact that Carnegie was not in Paris in 1903 when the offer was made does not detract from the theory that he might have provided the means for the committee which according to Aleister Crowley who met them in Ceylon, was composed of "genuine antiques with shaking heads, stooping shoulders, slobbering jaws from which hung white goatish beards, and bleared red eyes that blenched even in the twilight of the luncheon as if the very idea of sunlight was an infernal horror".[4] Crowley had come across them in the Grand Hotel Oriental in Colombo and, introducing himself as an Inverness laird, had offered his services. On hearing from them that the prosecution had the affidavits of seventy-seven witnesses to Macdonald's crime, he replied cheerily, "Ah, well. You don't know much of Ceylon. If there were seven times seventy-seven I wouldn't swing a cat on their dying oaths. The more unanimous they are, the more certain it is they have been bribed to lie."[5] A footnote by Crowley adds that Macdonald had upset the planters by ordering a "Ceylon Big Big" to leave a military occasion because he was in mufti. Presumably, Crowley, who lived in Ceylon for a time, was referring to the incident with the boys on the train, and to Macdonald's treatment of the Ceylon Militia. Although his story is condescendingly told and he lost interest in the committee thereafter, he is a pertinent witness to the notion that

Macdonald had been helped to destruction by the attitudes of high society on the island.

The committee's findings were published on 29th June 1903 and, predictably, they found Macdonald totally innocent and that the charges if they existed, were prompted only by jealousy.

> In reference to the grave charges made against the late Sir Hector Macdonald, we, the appointed and undersigned commissioners, individually and collectively, declare on oath that after the most careful, minute and exhaustive enquiry and investigation of the whole circumstances and facts connected with the sudden and unexpected death of the late Sir Hector Macdonald, unanimously and unmistakably find absolutely no reason or crime whatsoever which could create feelings such as would determine suicide, in preference to conviction of any crime affecting the moral and irreproachable character of so brave, so fearless, so glorious and unparalleled a hero; and we firmly believe the cause which gave rise to the INHUMAN and CRUEL suggestions of crime were prompted through vulgar feelings of SPITE and JEALOUSY in his rising to such a high rank of distinction in the British army; and while we have taken the most reliable and trustworthy evidence from every accessible and conceivable source, and have without hesitation come to the conclusion that there is not the visible, not the SLIGHTEST PARTICLE of Truth in foundation of any crime.
>
> (SIGNED) Angus Macdonald, Dr Matthew Wilson, Dr D. Macnaughton, James Brodie, Gerald Heathcote, Arthur Lang.[6]

That echo of the prejudices felt at home had no official standing and if the anonymous financier felt that his money had been well spent or no, he kept very quiet about the findings.

The only references to the commission in Ceylon came from a short-lived newspaper called *Native Opinion* which kept up a barrage of abuse against West Ridgeway. Throughout April it mounted a campaign to try to prove that Macdonald had fallen from grace due to Ridgeway's hostile attitudes and that the advice given to him to return to London was, in the event, ruinous to the general's career. The editors then changed their tack and criticised Ridgeway for his high caste attitudes, his lack of policies in Ceylon and for his inability to control his civil servants. They also hinted that the press in Ceylon were indeed in the Governor's pockets.

It is true that Ridgeway was a bad manager of people. Earlier, he had been determined to make an example of a Moslem from Batticoloa who, on being given a minor promotion, had presented Ridgeway with a present of fifty guineas, that being the going rate for petty corruption. An enraged Governor telegrammed Joseph Chamberlain about his decision to make an example of the man, and a sorry and bemused official found himself without a job. That Ridgeway had acted by the book is obvious, but a man of feeling might have been content with the return of the present and a minor rap over the knuckles. Lord Ampthill, a later governor, referred to the case while discussing Ridgeway's faults, and spoke of him as "being really hopeless".[7] There may be no way of proving that Ridgeway maltreated Macdonald—*Native Opinion's* views are too violent and opinionated to be considered completely trustworthy[8]—but his decision to sue the editors for libel in November, while understandable from a personal point of view, was hardly the done thing for a government official. "I propose to prosecute the editors for scurrilous articles on myself, in public capacity, under Section 120 of the Penal Code. If successful, the men will probably get rigorous imprisonment for some years, and above-mentioned conspiracy will be broken up. Do you approve? Case should be instituted before I leave."[9]

The officials in the Colonial Office in London hesitated before replying cautiously that the instigation of a case of that nature, involving libel, could only re-open the matter of Sir Hector Macdonald. Although their reasons for wanting to prevent that occurrence are not clear from the Colonial Office papers[10], two possiblities emerge: the first a genuine desire not to harm Macdonald's or the army's name further; and secondly and more likely, the growing realisation that the "affaire Macdonald" as it had become known, had been badly mishandled in Ceylon and in London. The official press rallied to Ridgeway's aid and the *Ceylon Observer* was particularly vociferous about the case as indeed it had been since the outset.

> Scotsmen are prone, like all humanity at times to accept the unwelcome as untrue, and in this case they were slow to discover that the feet of their idol were of clay. The thought of their martial hero sinking to rest unwept, unhonoured, and unsung, in an alien country, when all the circumstances were perfectly understood, was sufficient to give rise to the agitation for a Committee of Investigation. But we trust now that the grave has closed over the remains of the deceased, his countrymen will desist from clamouring for further details which can only intensify the pain which every Briton already feels.[11]

If Ridgeway had, in fact, done a deal with the press to preserve secrecy over the charges against Macdonald in the middle of March, he continued, too, to have their support until the end of the year when he left Ceylon, to be made a Privy Councillor in 1906 and to give further services to the Colonial Office in South Africa before his death in 1930.

Despite the outcry made by the editors of *Native Opinion*, and the findings of the commission, Ridgeway was not a mischief-maker, nor was he suited to that role. He may have misjudged the affair, but faced with what were to him, most terrible charges, made against the commander of the troops, he did his best to shield Macdonald, hoping that the War Office would post the general to some other, out-of-the-way part of the Empire. His statements to the Legislative Council, despite the protestations of Rasch and Weir, had to be made, although he could have chosen a more delicate wording—there was not a man in London who would have misunderstood the meaning of "grave charges". As for the idea that Ridgeway was additionally upset because his son was involved, it does not bear examination: Ridgeway's only child was a daughter. (see p. 138) Neither was it his fault that between them Macdonald and Roberts agreed that a return to Ceylon for court martial was the only way to clear Macdonald's name. The general may well have been unpopular in Ceylon as Ridgeway suggested but the allegations had substance to them and were not, as was commonly thought, borne of spite and jealousy.

Many Scots, who were unwilling to probe too deeply into the scandal, preferred instead to cast Kitchener in the role of traducer of Macdonald's fair name. Friends remembered Fighting Mac's veiled allusions to enemies in high places but these were uttered at a time when Macdonald was depressed and slightly paranoid. Kitchener's dispatches made generous mention of Macdonald and he in turn was no less inclined to speak well of his old boss. In Dingwall he had said, on receiving the freedom of the burgh, "There was nothing pleased me more, however, than the reference to my superior officer, Lord Kitchener of Khartoum. Were it not for his indomitable energy, there is no question that the Khartoum campaign would not have the successful issue which you now applaud. He it was who planned, and he it was who executed, and others were the simple instruments in his hands towards an end, and if we fulfilled his behests, all honour to him."

Perhaps, said others, Kitchener could not have liked the references made to Macdonald as the true hero of Omdurman by an ecstatic press, but Kitchener cared little about what newspapers had to say, and it is difficult to place too much credence on the belief that he and Macdonald fell out over the reports made by Steevens, Burleigh and Churchill, the last of whom he heartily detested. His only comment on Macdonald's suicide was a brief paragraph in reply to a letter from

Lord Roberts of 27th March. "What a sad ending it has been to
Macdonald. I never heard any rumour of the sort about him, but
Marker who has just joined me from Simla, says there is the same
story at Belgaum, of a similar nature; however, nothing is known,
only gossip."[12] Besides, the two men were old comrades, veterans of
the Sudan, and although Kitchener may have been a cold and aloof
man, he was loyal, in his own way, to his "band of boys". The fact
that Kitchener was probably latently homosexual has little bearing on
the case and I am inclined to the view first expressed by John
Montgomery[13], that Kitchener was in no position to arraign the friend
he had first met while virtuously in love with the doomed Hermione
Baker. Also, he was replete with honour in his own land and
commander-in-chief in India. What, we may ask, had he to fear from
a major-general in an inferior command like Ceylon? (Of course he
was ordered to provide the officers for the court martial, but that was
duty, not malice. Kitchener liked doing his duty.)

If the War Office was to blame—and they could have hushed up
the charges and given Macdonald another posting,—then most of it
must rest at the feet of Lord Roberts, the man who gave Fighting Mac
his chance and who had walked in and out of his life ever since. A
man possessed of a high moral code, Roberts expected much of his
officers, and in his own quirky, old-fashioned way, he looked for
much more from an officer of his favourite regiment, the Gordons.
Homosexual charges were bad enough, but those involving boys
were detestable. His letter of 27th March to Kitchener makes it quite
plain that he never had any intention of letting Macdonald off the
hook.

> You will have heard ere this of Macdonald's sad ending. Poor fellow.
> He wrote a letter from Paris, when he heard that the court martial had
> been ordered, saying he could never face it, and I felt sure he would
> disappear. I hoped that he might go to some out of the way part of the
> world, but having no means of his own, I suppose he thought it better
> to make away with himself. Ridgeway writes that there is great
> indignation in Ceylon at Macdonald having been sent there, as it is
> reported that there were similar scandals about him in South Africa
> and in India. I have been told since that there were grave suspicions
> about him when he was commanding at Aliwal North, and I have been
> wondering whether his anxiety to leave Belgaum was due to the same
> thing. He never ceased writing and telegraphing until I moved him to
> Ceylon.[14]

It was an attitude of indifference. A man in Macdonald's position
had to be seen to be honest and if that trust failed him there was only

one way to retrieve one's honour: to disprove the allegations or to surrender one's integrity. But even at that, Roberts was not being true to Macdonald. Earlier that year he had dealt with a homosexual scandal involving the Brigade of Guards and that had been hushed up, although Kitchener had expressed surprise at the Commander-in-Chief's decision. If the Guards could get away with it, could not the same have been done for Macdonald?

The answer must be, yes. If Macdonald had been possessed of influence in high places or indeed of more worldliness, or a guinea or two, then he could have taken legal or political advice and perhaps have put a damper on the charges. But he was, as Aleister Crowley described him, "a great, simple, lion-hearted man with the spirit of a child; with all his experience in the army, he still took the word honour seriously"[15]; and it was that implicit belief that took him back to Ceylon and to raise the pistol to his head in Paris once he saw that all was lost. What failed him was not so much his own faith in that concept, but society's faith in him. While he was a wartime soldier, stoutly defending the Empire with deeds of derring-do in faraway places, he was an acceptable hero, and if he was a ranker and not a gentleman then at least he knew how to fight. As a peacetime soldier he lacked finesse and had no exaggerated social graces, was strapped for cash and had no connections in high places. When he revealed his sexual tendencies and the fact that he liked little boys perhaps too much, then it all became clear. The whispers would have gone round the London clubs and the officers' messes, "What more can you expect from a chap with that sort of background?" By wiping the slate clean in room 105 in the Hotel Regina Macdonald was only doing his best to regain the army's trust in him, even if it was only in his memory, and thereafter, senior officers could say that poor old Mac had done the right thing.[16]

Macdonald's memory lingered on throughout the first decade of the new century until the First World War destroyed forever his own, and society's ideas about heroism. It is useless to contemplate his career had he lived: by the time of the Boer War his military techniques were already out of date and it is difficult to envisage how his belief in drill and discipline could have survived the Western Front. If he had lived through that holocaust—and many senior officers died in action— he would have lived to see post-war society yield little to the world fit for heroes. The British Army remained a preserve of outdated social snobberies and continued to betray many of the characteristics that Macdonald had encountered during his climb to a position of power. It would take another world war to blow the wind of change through its ranks, and that revolution was inspired by one of Macdonald's most strongly held beliefs: the existence of a conscript army.

Between 1948 and 1963, National Service gave British men the 'opportunity' of serving with the colours for a period of eighteen months, later made two years by the National Service Act of 1950. At the age of eighteen, conscripts were drafted into the three services, mainly into the army, and many saw service in Britain's remaining overseas commitments—Palestine, Malaya, Korea, Suez, Kenya and Cyprus. The army, in particular, did well out of the exercise, being able to pick and choose from a wide variety of recruits for its specialist arms, but there are doubts about the efficacy of conscription and its effects on the national servicemen. The arrival of the nuclear age had changed the face of modern warfare and although there was still a need for the infantryman, weapons were, on the whole, more sophisticated and tactics were constantly changing as Britain began the long retreat from Empire and started to look eastwards in Europe. Some national servicemen gained commissions, learned trades and benefitted from their two years' service, but as many politicians, Labour and Tory, looked on it as at best a means of coping with unemployment, or at worst as an alternative to borstal, it is small wonder that many remembered their time as "tedious, belittling, coarsening, brutalising, unjust and possibly psychologically very harmful".[17]

Today, the army is once again small, mobile and highly trained. Conditions are better, pay good, officers more democratically selected, a private can—in theory at least—become a general and with the spectre of mass unemployment haunting society, recruiting is not a problem. Homosexuality is one though. A soldier cannot remain in the service if he is homosexual and in January 1982 four soldiers were dismissed because of their sexual preferences. The news was barely reported in the press. Since the Wolfenden Report, which became law as the Sexual Offences Act of 1967 social attitudes towards homosexuality have changed for the better, even though it is still looked on as a security risk; but a major-general today who was also homosexual could not remain in a position of authority or discretion for long. There would be no need for him, perhaps, to blow out his brains and the social ostracism would be less than it was eighty years ago, but it would be a blot on his record. In that respect the army and society have changed little.

Other concepts have altered more dramatically. Honour, loyalty, heroism, discipline do not carry the same kudos as they did before the First World War and so a man like Macdonald, who revered those principles, may appear today as an antiquated, almost eccentric figure from a bygone age. But in his day those virtues were the lodestar of his life and the very fabric of his existence. A brave man to the last, his courage failed him not in the heat of battle but in the icy indifference of a class system that failed to stand by the hero of its own creation in his greatest hour of need.

Notes

Chapter Two—The Crofter's Son
1. Roger Taylor, *George Washington Wilson: Artist and Photographer* (Aberdeen 1981), 2
2. anon, *Hector Macdonald's Life Story* (n.d.), 10
3. quoted David Campbell, *General Sir Hector Macdonald*, (London 1900), 29
4. Hugh Miller, *My Schools and Schoolmasters* (Edinburgh 1854), 43
5. ibid, 45
6. Foulis Scrapbook, Dingwall Town Hall, 18
7. anon, op. cit., 9

Chapter Three—Off for a Soldier
1. P.C. Hoffman, *They Also Serve* (London 1949), 36
2. Thomas Jackson, *Narrative of the Eventful Life of Thomas Jackson, Late Sergeant of the Coldstream Guards* (Birmingham 1847), 86
3. C. Greenhill Gardyne, *The Life of a Regiment: The History of the Gordon Highlanders*, vol. 2, (London 1929), 292
4. anon, op. cit., 20
5. quoted Campbell, op. cit., 37–38
6. Victor Bonham-Carter, *Soldier True* (London 1963), 5
7. Foulis Scrapbook, op. cit., 3

Chapter Four—A Gay and Gallant Gordon
1. quoted James Morris, *Pax Britannica* (London 1968), 409
2. Frank Richards, *Old Soldier Sahib* (London 1966), 112
3. Greenhill Gardyne, op. cit., 96
4. ibid, 100

Chapter Five—Officer and Gentleman
1. Lord Roberts, *Forty-One Years in India* (London 1897),
2. Greenhill Gardyne, op. cit., 104
3. ibid, 104
4. Byron Farwell, *Queen Victoria's Little Wars* (London 1973), 208
5. Greenhill Gardyne, op. cit., 110
6. ibid, 110
7. ibid, 135
8. Corelli Barnett, *Britain and Her Army* (London 1970), 315
9. Bonham-Carter, op. cit., 32
10. Corelli Barnett, op. cit., 314
11. Greenhill Gardyne, op. cit., 143

Chapter Six—**Remember Majuba!**

1. Ian B. Hamilton, *The Happy Warrior: A Life of Sir Ian Hamilton* (London 1966), 19
2. Ian Hamilton, *Listening for the Drums* (London 1944), 69
3. Wolseley Papers, Wolseley to Hicks Beach 28th October 1879
4. J.H. Settle, *Anecdotes of Soldiers in Peace and War* (London 1905), 309
5. quoted Campbell, 70
6. Greenhill Gardyne, op. cit., 170–171
7. ibid, 164
8. quoted Campbell, 72
9. Ian B. Hamilton, op. cit., 42

Chapter Seven—**On the Strength**

1. Settle, op. cit., 309
2. Greenhill Gardyne, op. cit., 238
3. Kenneth I.E. Macleod, *The Ranker* (Cortland, N.Y. 1976), 19
4. Foulis Scrapbook, op. cit., 47
5. Macleod, op. cit., 50
6. William Acton, *Functions and Disorders of the Reproductive Organs* 6th ed. (London 1875), 64
7. anon, *Low Life in Victorian Edinburgh* (Edinburgh 1980), 127
8. Richards, op. cit., 199
9. J.M. Barrie, *The Little White Bird* (London 1902), 6
10. quoted Derek Hudson, *Lewis Carroll: An Illustrated Biography* (London 1976), 216
11. Dora Langlois, *The Child: Its Origin and Development* (London 1896), 27

Chapter Eight—**What an Accursed Country!**

1. Charles Chenevix Trench, *Charley Gordon: An Eminent Victorian Reassessed* (London 1978), 64
2. Lord Edward Cecil, *Leisure of an Egyptian Official* (London 1921), 184
3. see Major-General Frank Richardson, *Mars Without Venus: A Study of Some Homosexual Generals* (Edinburgh 1981), 117–126; Sir Philip Magnus, *Kitchener: Portrait of an Imperialist* (London 1958), 10; George H. Cassar, *Kitchener: Architect of Victory* (London 1977), 95–98 for a fuller discussion of this topic.
4. Magnus, op. cit., 81
5. Cyril Pearl, *Morrison of Peking* (London 1967), 200
6. ibid, 103
7. Sir Alfred Milner, *England in Egypt* (London 1895), 147
8. G.W. Steevens, *With Kitchener to Khartoum* (London 1899), 57
9. ibid, 58
10. Bennet Burleigh, *Khartoum Campaign* (London 1899), 75

Chapter Nine—**Omdurman**

1. quoted Morris, op. cit., 245
2. Steevens, op. cit., 89
3. quoted Magnus, op. cit., 99
4. Kitchener Papers, Kitchener to Foreign Office, 10th April 1898
5. quoted Magnus, op. cit., 134

6. Bennet Burleigh, *Sirdar and Khalifa, or the reconquest of the Sudan* (London 1898), 135
7. ibid.
8. Steevens, op. cit., 263
9. Burleigh, *Khartoum Campaign*, op. cit., 186
10. Steevens, op. cit., 278
11. Winston Churchill, *The River War* (London 1899), 137
12. Burleigh, *Khartoum Campaign*, op. cit., 193

Chapter Ten—Scotia's Darling
1. Winston Churchill, to his mother, 8th October 1898
2. Burleigh, *Khartoum Campaign*, op. cit., 284
3. Kitchener Papers, Kitchener to Foreign Office, 5th September 1898
4. quoted Campbell, op. cit., 101
5. Thomas F.G. Coates, *Hector Macdonald* (London 1900), 23
6. ibid, 10

Chapter Eleven—Fighting Mac!
1. Rudyard Kipling, 'Three and an Extra', from *Plain Tales from the Hills* (London 1964), 17
2. Byron Farwell, op. cit., 342
3. quoted, W. Baring Pemberton, *Battles of the Boer War* (London 1972) 105
4. Arthur Conan Doyle, *The Great Boer War* (London 1900), 308
5. *Black and White*, 10th March 1900
6. quoted Foulis Scrapbook, op. cit., 9
7. ibid., 13
8. ibid., 5
9. quoted David L. Cromb, *Hector Macdonald* (Stirling 1903), 109
10. Kitchener Papers, Macdonald to Kitchener, 26th January 1900
11. quoted Byron Farwell, *The Great Boer War* (London 1977), 366
12. Roberts Papers, Roberts to Kitchener, 27th March 1903; Kitchener Papers, Kitchener to Roberts, 20th April 1903
13. Roberts Papers, Roberts to Kitchener, 5th April 1901

Chapter Twelve—Pro Consul
1. *Melbourne Argus*, 12th October, 1902
2. Frank Harris, *Oscar Wilde* (London 1938), 171
3. for a full discussion see H. Montgomery Hyde, *The Other Love: An Historical and Contemporary Survey of Homosexuality in Britain* (London 1970), 110-120; Ronald Pearsall, *The Worm in the Bud: The World of Victorian Sexuality* (London 1969), 452–456
4. Hyde, op. cit., 110
5. Leonard Woolf, *Diaries in Ceylon, 1904–1911* (London 1960), xiv–xv
6. Morris, op. cit., 222–223
7. Richard Meinertzhagen, *Army Diary, 1899–1926* (Edinburgh and London 1960), 24
8. Macleod, *The Ranker*, op. cit., 19–20
9. Woolf, 'A Tale Told by Moonlight', op. cit., 264

Chapter Thirteen—'Grave, very grave charges'
1. In his novel *Fighting Mac* (London 1977) William Clive arranges for Macdonald to enjoy the friendship of a native boy, Kiri Lamaya
2. Colonial Office Papers, Ridgeway to Colonial Office, in CO 537/410, 537/411 and 54/686.
3. Quoted in John Montgomery, 'The Truth about Fighting Mac', *Gay News*, 150, 24
4. Colonial Office Papers, Ridgeway to Colonial Office, 19th February 1903.
5. *Ceylon Observer*, 20th February 1903
6. quoted in several Scottish newspapers, Foulis scrapbook, op. cit., 34
7. Colonial Office Papers, Sir E.W. Ward to Ridgeway, 19th March 1903
8. Roberts Papers, Roberts to Kitchener, 19th March 1903
9. Harris, op. cit., 153
10. Aleister Crowley, *Confessions*, ed. John Symonds, (London 1969), 383
11. quoted in *The Times*, 26th March 1903
12. *The Scotsman*, 27th March 1903

Chapter Fourteen—Not a Drum was Heard
1. *The Scotsman*, 25th March 1903
2. William Thom, *The Idol of the Scottish Nation*, pamphlet of Edinburgh, April 1903, copy in the National Library of Scotland.
3. *The Scotsman*, 5th April 1903
4. C.W. Hill, *Edwardian Scotland* (Edinburgh and London 1976), 153

Chapter Fifteen—Von Mackensen and Other Myths
1. John Montgomery, *Toll for the Brave* (London 1963), 178– 179
2. *Aberdeen Press and Journal*, 7th March 1977
3. Macleod, *The Ranker*, op. cit., 51
4. ibid, 52
5. G.A. Minto, 'Two Lives or One?' *Blackwoods Magazine*, June 1962, 493
6. Hyde, op. cit., 173
7. Story told to author by Major-General Frank Richardson
8. Wolfgang Förster, *Mackensen: Briefe und Aufzeichungen* (Leipzig 1938), 9
9. J. Keagan and A. Wheatcroft, *Who's Who in Military History* (London 1976), 'Von Mackensen',204
10. George P. Gooch, *Before the War*, vol.1 (London 1936), 56

Chapter Sixteen—Aftermath
1. Robert Service, *Songs of a Sourdough* (London 1962), 103
2. Hansard, 1st April 1903
3. Reported in several Scottish newspapers.
4. Crowley, op. cit., 384
5. ibid, 384
6. from a document in the author's possession.
7. Colonial Office Papers 54/666, Ampthill to Chamberlain
8. For a more sympathetic account of the *Native Opinion* case, see Macleod, *A Victim of Fate*, 8–24
9. Colonial Office Papers, 54/686, Ridgeway to Chamberlain

10. Colonial Office Papers, CO 537/410, 537/411, 54/686
11. *Ceylon Observer*, 3rd April 1903
12. Kitchener Papers, Kitchener to Roberts, 20th April 1903
13. Montgomery, op. cit., 139–140
14. Roberts Papers, Roberts to Kitchener, 27th March 1903
15. Crowley, op. cit., 384
16. Richardson, op. cit., 123
17. B.S. Johnson (ed.) *All Bull: The National Servicemen* (London 1973), 14

Select Bibliography and Further Reading

I

During his lifetime, two biographies were written about Sir Hector Macdonald. Both were published in 1900 and contain much similar anecdotal material told in a breathlessly narrated *Boy's Own Paper* style. They are David Campbell's *General Sir Hector Macdonald: The Story of a Romantic Career* and Thomas F.G. Coates' *Hector Macdonald: A Highland Laddie's Life and Laurels*. After his death in 1903 appeared David L. Cromb's short biographical sketch, *Hector Macdonald*, which reproduces many of the letters and newspaper reports that followed hard upon the burial in Edinburgh. It is also rich in anecdotes relating to the general, especially from the Boer War period. There were, too, several anonymous lives of Macdonald published in later magazines but they rely heavily on the three first biographies. Sixty years were to pass before the publicaton of John Montgomery's *Toll for the Brave: The Tragedy of Sir Hector Macdonald* (1963), a readable study that attempted to analyse Macdonald's homosexuality and which also defused much of the passion many felt about Kitchener's attitudes to Fighting Mac's downfall. Montgomery also dealt with G.A. Minto's June 1962 article, 'Two Lives or One' which appeared in *Blackwood's Magazine* and which had suggested that Macdonald had assumed the identity of Field Marshal von Mackensen. A Gaelic biography, *Eachunn nan Cath* ('Hector of the Battles') by Allan Fraser (1979) dealt with the plain facts of Macdonald's life; and in 1976 and in 1978 respectively, appeared Kenneth I.E. Macleod's pamphlets, *The Ranker* and *A Victim of Fate*, both of which were the result of the author's patient researches in London and Ceylon. His earlier work on Macdonald had appeared as a serial, 'High Endeavour' in the *North Star* newspaper between 1949 and 1950. Macdonald has also been the subject of a novel, *Fighting Mac* (1977), by William Clive, who is better known for the creation of the fictional Victorian soldier, Private Dando; and there have been two dramatisations of Fighting Mac's life. The first was published in Australia in 1944. Written by J. Beresford Fowler and Sylvia Archer, it suggested that Macdonald's downfall was due to his friendship with the sons of a Burgher family. More successful was Donald Mackenzie's play, *Fighting Mac* which was performed at the Traverse Theatre, Edinburgh in January 1978 after being produced as an earlier radio play on BBC Radio Scotland. In 1976, BBC TV Scotland produced a documentary about Sir Hector, directed by James Wilson, with Ian Cuthbertson as narrator; and in 1982, STV produced their own documentary film, written by the present author and directed by Archie McArthur.

II

The other principal books consulted were:

Amery, L.S., *The Times History of the War in South Africa, 1899–1900*, 7 vols., London, 1900–1909

Alleridge, Hilliard, *Towards Khartoum*, London, 1897

Barnett, Corelli, *Britain and her Army 1509–1970*, London, 1970

Burleigh, Bennet, *Sirdar and Khalifa, or the Reconquest of the Sudan*, London 1898; *Khartoum Campaign 1898*, London, 1899

Cassar, George H., *Kitchener: Architect of Victory*, London, 1977

Churchill, Winston, *The River War*, London, 1899
  My Early Life, London, 1959

Chenevix Trench, Charles, *Charley Gordon*, London, 1978

Doyle, Arthur Conan, *The Great Boer War*, London , 1900

Dupuy, Ernest R., and Trevor, *The Encyclopaedia of Military History*, London, 1970

Farwell, Byron, *Queen Victoria's Little Wars*, London, 1973
  The Great Boer War, London, 1977

Förster, Wolfgang, *Mackensen: Briefe und Aufzeichungen des Generalfeldmarschall aus Krieg und Frieden*, Leipzig, 1938

Fortescue, John, *The Empire and the Army*, London, 1928

Gardyne, C. Greenhill, *The Life of a Regiment: The History of the Gordon Highlanders*, vol. 2, London, 1929

Hamilton, Ian, *Listening for the Drums*, London, 1944

Hamilton, Ian B., *The Happy Warrior: A Life of General Sir Ian Hamilton*, London, 1966

Harvie, Christopher, *Scotland and Nationalism, Scottish Society and Politics 1707–1977*, London, 1977

Hill, C.W., *Edwardian Scotland*, Edinburgh and London, 1976

Hyde, H. Montgomery, *The Other Love: An Historical and Contemporary Account of Homosexuality in Britain*, London, 1970

James, David, *Lord Roberts*, London, 1954

Kruger, Rayne, *Goodbye Dolly Gray*, London, 1959

Laffin, John, *Scotland the Brave*, London 1963

Lehmann, Joseph, *All Sir Garnet*, London 1964
  The First Boer War, London, 1972

Lord, John, *Duty, Honour, Empire*, London, 1971

Luyken, Max, *Generalfeldmarschall von Mackensen: von Bukarest bis Saloniki*, Munich, 1920

Magnus, Philip, *Kitchener: Portrait of an Imperialist*, London 1958

Milner, Alfred, *England in Egypt*, London, 1892

Morris, James, *Pax Britannica: Climax of Empire*, London 1968

Pearsall, Ronald, *The Worm in the Bud: The World of Victorian Sexuality*, London 1969

Pemberton, W. Baring, *Battles of the Boer War*, London, 1964

Richards, Frank, *Old Soldier Sahib*, London, 1966

Richardson, F.M., *Fighting Spirit: Psychological Factors in War*, London 1978
  Mars Without Venus: A Study of some Homosexual Generals, Edinburgh 1981

Roberts, Lord, *Forty-One Years in India*, 2 vols., London, 1897
Robertson, Sir William, *From Private to Field Marshal*, London, 1921
Robinson, Charles N., (ed.), *Celebrities of the British Army*, London, 1900
Rogers, H.C.B., *Weapons of the British Soldier*, London, 1960
Royle, Charles, *The Egyptian Campaigns 1882 and 1885*, London 1900
Selby, John, *The Boer War: A Study in Cowardice and Courage*, London, 1969
Sinclair-Stevenson, Christopher, *The Gordon Highlanders*, London, 1968
Steevens, G.W., *With Kitchener to Khartoum*, Edinburgh and London, 1899
Trudgill, Eric, *Madonnas and Magdalens: The Origins and Development of Victorian Sexual Attitudes*, London, 1976
West, D.J., Roy, C., Nicols, F.L., *Understanding Sexual Attacks*, Cambridge, 1978
Woolf, Leonard, *Diaries in Ceylon, 1904–1911*, London, 1960
Ziegler, Philip, *Omdurman*, London, 1973
Zulfo, Ismat Hasan, *Karari*, London, 1980

Index